George Douglas Campbell Argyll

The New British Constitution and its Master-Builders

George Douglas Campbell Argyll

The New British Constitution and its Master-Builders

ISBN/EAN: 9783337397258

Printed in Europe, USA, Canada, Australia, Japan

Cover: Foto ©ninafisch / pixelio.de

More available books at **www.hansebooks.com**

THE NEW BRITISH

CONSTITUTION

AND ITS

MASTER-BUILDERS

BY THE

DUKE OF ARGYLL

EDINBURGH:

DAVID DOUGLAS

1888

CONTENTS.

PART I.

OUR OLD CONSTITUTION : HOW IT STOOD AND GREW.

CONTENTS

PART II.

CONTENTS.

APPENDIX.

PART I.

OUR OLD CONSTITUTION:

HOW IT STOOD AND GREW.

———◆———

THE name Dissentient Liberals was, I believe,
selected by Mr. Gladstone, in a moment of comparative moderation, as the simplest name for
those former associates who have refused to follow
him in his new Irish policy. Simple it certainly
is, and perhaps comparatively inoffensive. But
it is by no means colourless. Like many other
names it has a good deal in it. It savours of
authority, and of some established teaching. It
assumes a standard of assent and consent from
which the Dissentients have dissented. What
the standard is from which they have departed
is a question well worth the asking. I desire
to push this question here — and the further
question—what those doctrines are by which we

A

continue to abide. Disclaiming any right to speak for others, I recognise the present as a supreme moment in which we are all bound to speak, and to speak freely.

The grammar of our assent has been a grammar of intelligible rules. Like other sound rules of conduct and of belief, they rest, to a large extent, not on opinion but on fact. And foremost among these facts is this—that we live under a Constitution which, as a whole, has never been reduced to writing. Its marches and its outlines are elastic—in some places hardly visible, because they have never been absolutely fixed. No walls of stone enclose it. No circuit of entrenched posts confine it. So far as mere mechanical contrivances are concerned it is an undefended city. It is a Constitution, nevertheless, on which everything depends—all the more for the very reason that it is not a document, nor a statute, nor even a code. It is far more than any of these—it is a vast body of accepted doctrines, accumulated, sifted, selected, and transmitted through more than a thousand years. Its teachings are our universal preconceptions, the background of all our conduct and opinions. In every sphere of public duty, whether it be large or small—in the discharge of every public function, however local and comparatively unimportant, we are governed from one imperial centre of tradition and of law. We are often unconscious how much we owe to it. In the light of it our very ideas of liberty have been formed. It restrains and guides us in the exercise of power where power has been intrusted to us. It defends and guards us where we are ourselves subject to authority. Yet, except for the hold its precepts have over our instincts and affections, it is wholly unprotected. Every part of it is at the mercy of ordinary legislation. The process which passes a road act, or delegates to some parochial authority the power of making sewers, is the same process exactly which is competent to subvert the Monarchy, to break up the constitution of Parliament, to confer arbitrary powers upon local majorities, and to prostrate all personal liberties under the feet of the village tyrant.

We take note of these facts, and we deduce from them an important lesson. They bring home to us what political leadership under such a system is, or ought to be. It is the function of leaders to represent and to interpret better than other men such opinions, and tendencies of opinion, as commend themselves to the intellect and conscience of those who follow. Authority, properly so called, they have none. That is to say, it is not their function to declare—it is not our duty to accept—anything to be wise and true simply because it may suddenly be convenient to them to say it is so. It is our duty to be jealous of any claim of this kind, and to watch every departure from doctrines of established value or of immemorial acceptance. Especially is it our duty to bring to the test of our own old political instincts—of our own rich inheritance of political thought—every marked or unexpected change of policy, and every new dexterous stroke of tactics. It should never be forgotten that, more than most men, perhaps most of all men, party leaders in the game of politics are exposed to violent temptation—from passions which in themselves are natural, and from the abundant covering of conscious motives which may be good. Above all, we must bear constantly in mind the tremendous issues which may be at stake on the cards they play.

We affirm that such is our position now. We see with certainty that the questions involved in the new Irish policy are questions which go to the very centres of our political life. The curious fact that Mr. Gladstone on a late memorable occasion cavilled at the words which reckoned the Act of Union among our 'fundamental laws,' was an ominous fact in our eyes, and full of warning. If the contention be that there is no Act which cannot be altered or repealed by the same authority which passed it, we admit the fact, and we know all the significance of the admission. But if it means, or if it even hints, that in our constitutional system there are no laws which can be called fundamental in the truest sense, then we not only deny it, but we regard it with just suspicion. It must be a most attractive doctrine to a great party leader, that there is nothing which he may not touch and handle as freely as he may think expedient or may find convenient, no settlement which he may not unsettle, no inheritance which he may not put up to auction. It is not any mechanical contrivance of any kind—it is not any mere outward fortification of method and of process—

which makes one law fundamental and another not. The difference lies in the nature of things. History may determine it, in so far as historical events are the index of causes deeper than themselves. In all human structures there are parts on which the whole depends—parts for resisting pressure, for supporting weight, for dividing strain, for concentrating and directing force. And so it is with political constitutions. In the growth and development of our own there have been memorable epochs when the strain has been tremendous, and when the nation has laboured under a sense of immediate danger. The outgrowths of those times have been, and are, amongst our most fundamental laws. They are like the special buttress-roots which healthy trees throw out in special situations of exposure, or like the strong adapted structures which many higher organisms have developed in response to needs, for the maintenance of their stability and for the continuance of their life.

We are consentient with all those former generations which have lived in the critical epochs of our national life, and have stood the brunt of its heavy storms. As we look back upon its history we can feel almost with a shudder what the danger sometimes was; and we can appreciate the rest, and peace, and progress, which followed on the noble work that was done to meet it.

In particular we recognise the fact that one of the greatest dangers of all has been the danger of disunion from separate races diverging into separate nationalities, with separate passions and separate ambitions. The struggles and efforts through which this danger has been averted have strained to the very utmost the powers of our greatest men. They have tested in an equal degree the highest political instincts of our people. In Scotland the best of our early Kings had to deal with, and formally to address, some four or five separate races, each, more or less, with a local habitation and a name—each jealous of the other—each differing in origin, in laws, in language, and in religion, and all of them for a long period jealous of the central power. Some natural causes of gradual interfusion assisted in our escape; but in the main it was effected under the fire of war, and by the spirit evoked under one heroic leader. The Monarchy—the Nation which was restored at Bannockburn was restored by union. All our tribes—all our races were represented in the army of Bruce—French, Normans and Angles, Scots and Galwegians, Celts and Saxons. · Yet for 300 years the tendency to division, the ambition of petty clans, and the pride of petty islands, kept up a perpetual revolt against the national standard of civilisation and of law.

When the western Celts were finally subdued under the central government, a large area of country was redeemed from a local barbarism of the most desolating kind. And when providentially the two Crowns of England and Scotland were united, the twin blessings of peace and of the expansion of industry were felt for the first time for centuries over the whole country south of the Clyde and Forth, and north of the Solway and the Tyne. But a still more signal proof of the danger involved in separating institutions was yet to come. Perhaps there never were two populations so bound together in natural affinities, in common geographical relations, and in mutual interests, as the people of England and of Scotland. Yet the mere union of the Crowns was powerless to make them feel it. In some ways it even aggravated jealousies and antagonisms. These were embodied and exasperated by the inevitable working of two separate Parliaments, until at last jealousy and rivalry were hardening into antipathy, and the two nations were actually arming for a desperate civil war. It is not improbable that a plebiscite would have rejected Union, on both sides the border. Most fortunately the voice of the cultivated classes was then powerful enough to be predominant ; and we owe to a comparatively small group of wise and enlightened men that union which opened to Scotland those wide horizons of enterprise and prosperity on which her sons were not slow to enter, and in which they have done so much.

Dangers exactly the same in kind were developed in Ireland out of the same causes. And the result was all the more remarkable in this case, because Ireland never possessed the separate elements of nationality which Scotland had possessed for centuries. Ireland as a whole never had a Sovereign, nor a Capital, nor a central Government of its own. Yet in a very few years after the concession of independent powers had been made in favour of its separate Parliament, the centrifugal forces which such Institutions must always tend to generate, had led to differences on vital questions. The sense of imminent danger in Great Britain was instinctive and almost universal. The members of a professional opposition of course opposed. But they were a mere handful of men, and when in the course of years these very men survived the great Minister who carried the Union, and themselves came into office and into power, no sound ever came from them that was not in harmony with that universal acquiescence which is the sign and seal of all our fundamental laws. It is a signal homage to this national acquiescence that the leader in the new policy deprecates and denies the accusation that it would repeal the Union. I do not stop now even for a moment to bring this denial to a test. It has at any rate a high value for our present purpose as a witness to the national memory of the dangers which arose from a separate Parliament in Ireland. It bows before that memory and assumes to share it.

But the denial that Mr. Gladstone's scheme was a repeal of the Union, valuable as it is for this purpose, is still more valuable for another. Whether his bills were more or less than a repeal of the Union, it is at least certain that they were not repeal pure and simple. That is to say, they would not have left us where we were before the Act of Union. They would neither have restored the Grattan Parliament as it was, nor the constitution of Ireland as it was regulated before the transactions of 1782. If the denial that his Bills would have been any repeal of the Union, means only that they would not have restored anything ever known before, then indeed the denial is a just one. It is quite true that the scheme of those Bills was novel—absolutely novel. The Constitution it would have set up was not like anything ever heard of before either in this country or in any other.

Consentient as we are with all the experience and all the traditions of our country on the risks involved in separate Parliaments, and on the imminent dangers which we know that we escaped by Union, we are not less consentient with our former colleagues in recognising the fact that they have presented us with something new—something on which they have doubtless spent much of what is called thought, ability, and ingenuity.

But this is one of the very facts upon which we take at least a preliminary stand. We say

that this is not the method by which the British
Constitution has been elaborated.   Never since
our earliest history has any group of men seated
themselves round a green table, and .drawn up out
of their inner consciousness for the English, or for
the British people, a new political constitution.
From first to last our political system, all our
ideas touching it, and even the very channels in
which they run, have been inherited.   Our very
Revolutions have been effected in the name of
well-known and ancient rights.   From the meeting
of the Barons on the famous meadow in the valley
of the Thames—through the Reformation—through
the Revolution and the change of Dynasty, down
to the Union of the Parliaments, everything has
been done on old and familiar lines.   If there be
any exception, perhaps the nearest approach to it
is in that Act of the Irish Parliament which
claimed and set up in Ireland an independent
Legislature.   The Statute of Geo. i. which in
1719 asserted the supremacy of the Parliament of
Great Britain was strictly a Declaratory Act.   It
asserted the British supremacy as one that had
been, that was, and that ought to be—one that
the British Parliament 'had, hath, and of right

ought to have.' These are the words employed.[1]
And although the Irish Parliament in 1782 based
its proceedings on a Declaration of Right, it did
not seek to extract from the British Parliament
any retractation of its former historical claim or
of its historical assertion.[2]   The Constitution set
up by Grattan's Parliament was unquestionably
more nearly an absolute novelty than any other of
the changes through which we have passed.   The
evils and dangers to which it led, in spite of the
limited and well-affected classes who were alone
intrusted with its powers, are a great lesson on
the difficulty of foreseeing or controlling the in-
herent forces which underlie political organisation.
These forces, unless they have cut their own course,
and found their own bed, are not easily restrained.
They are quite sure to burst and break through all
restrictions that are purely forensic and artificial.

When, therefore, Mr. Gladstone denies that his
scheme repeals the Union, we ask whether it does
less or whether it does a great deal more.   The
first answer must be, at any rate, that it does something entirely different—something wholly beyond

[1] 6 Geo. I. cap. v.
[2] Lecky's *History of England*, vol. iv. p. 553.

and beside its effect upon the Act of 1800. It is not a matter of opinion but a matter of fact that it abolishes the United Parliament. It is not a matter of opinion but of fact that it creates not only a separate Irish Parliament but a separate Irish Executive, which has never before existed. Nor is it open to dispute that the scheme raises by inevitable consequence the most difficult abstract questions on the definition of matters which are to be subject, or not subject, to legislation by one Parliament or the other—on the relations of the new Executive to an Imperial authority—on the guarantees which must, or which need not, be required for the protection of life, of personal liberty, and of property.

On all these most difficult and complicated questions everything is to depend on the wide vision and the practical skill of the framers of one great organic law. No such work as this has ever before been undertaken by the statesmen of the United Kingdom or of any part of it. Those who devised the Acts of Union with Scotland in 1707 and with Ireland in 1800, did not attempt and had no need to attempt any such ambitious undertaking. All they had to do was to provide

for the complete amalgamation of two legisla-
latures into one. Equal participation in common
rights and privileges—immemorially known, and
needing no definitions—was the basis and the
essence of their plan. No new Constitution was
required. The two legislatures of the two kingdoms were added to the legislature of the third,
each acquiring its own full share of power in a
long-established political system, and over an
United Empire. Both these Unions were great
acts, both were in their nature and effects fundamental laws. But both of them were perfectly
simple in their nature. They got rid of complications, most dangerous and intricate complications.
But they invented none. Not the slightest change
was contemplated or effected in the principles of
the Constitution. No new organic statute was
even dreamed of, no evoking of new forces and
new ambitions, with weapons placed in new hands
for ready use, and then, with elaborate and ingenious contrivances, on paper, which pretend to
regulate and control them.

We take note again of these differences, amount-
ing to antitheses, between the new Irish policy
and everything of which we or our ancestors have

had experience. We observe, too, that the propounder of this policy has admitted both its character of organic change, and its character of absolute novelty, as regards the mind and intellect of the people. He declares it as a subject 'which goes down to the very roots and foundations of our whole civil and political constitution,' [1] and, again, as 'a subject which twelve months ago was almost as foreign to the British mind as the differential calculus.' [2]

This is true in one sense ; but in another sense it is most erroneous. It is perfectly true that the subject is one going down to the very roots of all we have known and loved in our Political Institutions. It is perfectly true also that there is no precedent for our present position respecting it. But the absolute novelty in our situation does not lie in the subject, but in the method of dealing with it proposed by Mr. Gladstone. The proposal to revive a separate Parliament in Ireland is not new. It has been before our people—at one time as a very burning question—far more than half-a-century. It is now fifty-five years since it

---

[1] *History of an Idea*, p. 20.
[2] *Ibid.; Lessons of the Elections*, p. 38.

formed the subject of an emphatic paragraph in the Speech from the Throne, and the Minister who wrote that speech was the very man who had been one of the chief critics of Mr. Pitt in his Act of Union. Earl Grey was a firm opponent of O'Connell's agitation. He put into the mouth of the Sovereign, on a very solemn occasion, in 1834, a declaration that the Legislative Union with Ireland was the 'bond of our national strength and safety,' and a repeated assurance to the United Parliament that 'it was his fixed and unalterable resolution, under the blessing of Divine Providence, to maintain it inviolate by all means in his power.'[1]

The Ministry in which Mr. Gladstone began his public life, the great Ministry of Sir Robert Peel, met that agitation by most unusual exertions of executive authority. Ever since, the demand for a separate Parliament in Ireland has been treated by every responsible statesman in Britain as absolutely inadmissible. The subject, therefore, in its essential character, was not foreign to the British mind. Several times it had been urgently pressed upon the attention of the public, and it was never absent from the mind of instructed men.

[1] *Mirror of Parliament*, vol. i. p. 2.

B

They knew, all of them, by instinct as well as by reasoning, that the re-erection of a separate Parliament in Ireland would and must involve the most complicated novelties of political organisation. The analogue, in respect to novelty, of the differential calculus, is to be found not in the policy in which all British Statesmen have been consentient since 1800—for that has been thoroughly thought out, and was perfectly familiar—but in the new-fangled schemes for deserting that policy which have been suddenly devised by Mr. Gladstone.   I do not say that we are consentient with Mr. Gladstone in this national instinct, for we did not look to any leader in such a matter.   He was consentient with us—meaning by 'us' not only the Liberal party, but all parties in the British Parliament.

We are consentient with our former leader even now, when he gives the name of a 'new formula' to the revised proposal for a separate Irish Parliament, which arose about 1871, under the new name of Home Rule, and under the auspices of Mr. Butt.[1]   This is exactly what it was—a new formula and nothing more.   It was regarded by us all as simply our old enemy with

---

[1] *History of an Idea*, pp. 12, 13.

a new face. It was Repeal under a new name. We knew, as Mr. Gladstone also did, that it involved, and must of necessity involve, 'either undoing or modifying the present Constitution of the Imperial Parliament.'[1] We knew, as he did, that it was a demand for the 'breaking up of the existing constitution of the Legislature.'[2] When our then leader paid the compliment to Mr. Butt of acknowledging that he did not demand a severance from the Crown of the United Kingdom,— ' that the Union of these kingdoms under her Majesty was to be maintained,'—we never for a moment supected the interpretation now put upon it, that he was 'admitting that the idea of Home Rule was not in its essence destructive of the unity of the Empire.'[3] We had not the smallest reason to suspect anything of the sort. We knew that the old agitators for Repeal had never openly avowed a desire to throw off the mere supremacy of the Crown. Mr. Butt was not shifting his ground one inch from the old basis of Repeal in giving the same assurance. Neither could we suspect that our leader, in 'accepting' it, was abating one jot of the argument on

---

[1] *History of an Idea*, pp. 12, 13. [2] *Ibid.* p. 13. [3] *Ibid.* pp. 13, 14.

which Repeal had always been resisted as inadmissible. I mean that so far as our knowledge went, or as his words naturally went, he was making no such abatement. We have nothing to do with what he intended at the time, or with any *ex post facto* interpretation he may now put on his own words. The context made their natural meaning plain enough, because the essence of that context was to point out the profound distinction between a union depending only on the link of a common Crown, and the existing Union depending on the whole constitution of the Legislature. He put this antithesis emphatically, and most formidably, when he described Mr. Butt's proposal as involving a demand ' that Parliament was to be broken up.' [1]

But our consentience since 1871 has not been confined to this formidable and just description of what the ' new formula ' really meant. The breaking up of a great Parliamentary Constitution never can be otherwise than a tremendous experiment. But there are conditions under which, at least, the most extreme forms of danger might not be imminent. If the parts of a united nation which are to be re-sundered into separate parliaments, are

[1] *History of an Idea*, p. 14.

agreed upon the fundamental laws of human Society concerning the security of life, of property, and of personal freedom, then the work of framing a new constitution for keeping them together, however arduous, or even perilous, would not be hopeless.   But this is exactly the condition which, as a matter of fact, has been wanting in the case of Ireland.   There has always been an obscure, but constant and close, connection between Irish political agitation and Irish lawlessness and crime.   Irish agitators had been always more or less disloyal, not merely to the political connection with Great Britain, but to the moral and physical connection between law and the enforcement of all social rights, duties, and obligations.   Jacobinism had been one main element in the Rebellion of 1798.   The French Directory had been invited to send its revolutionary army into Ireland ; and when it landed, an Irishman had issued assignats for the Province of Connaught.   It was the object of all the wise men who promoted the Union, to resist more effectually both foreign enemies and domestic anarchy.

The memory of this connection had never died out among us. It had been kept alive from time to time, down to what Mr. Gladstone calls the ' merging ' of

Repeal into the 'dangerous conspiracy' of Fenian-ism,[1] by recurring outbursts of crime, euphoniously described as 'partial and lawless action.'[2]   It had all the force and effect of an inseparable association. Nothing had occurred in 1871 to give any of us a new impression.   On the contrary the 'new formula' was heralded by the old accompaniments.   It was the conviction of us all that the new Irish Party desired a separate Parliament, in order to effect through it measures of oppression and injustice, which no Imperial Parliament, with its imperial traditions of justice and of law, could be easily got to sanction.

Now it is undeniable that often during the fifteen years between 1871 and the general election of 1885 Mr. Gladstone was consentient with us, and we were consentient with him, both in language and in action, which had no other justification than in our continued belief that the 'new formula' contemplated not only the breaking up the machinery of Parliament, but also the breaking up of the accepted doctrines of civilised society on the securities to be provided for life, liberty, and property.   This was a separate fact

[1] *History of an Idea*, p. 10.   [2] *Ibid.* p. 9.

which did far more than merely aggravate and intensify the objection to the breaking up of Parliament. It gave to that objection a very special force and character. It obviously imported into the work of forming a new legislative system, dangers, complications, and difficulties of the most formidable nature.

Now it is very remarkable that during the fifteen years referred to we were all consentient in doings and in sayings which dwelt more and more emphatically on this feature of the case. In Mr. Gladstone's speech at Aberdeen in September 1871, he was content with setting forth in the strongest language the formidable magnitude of the proposals necessarily involved in the 'new formula,' without any allusion to the specially aggravating conditions in the case of Ireland. This part of the work he did well. He called it a demand that 'Ireland should close her relations with the Parliament of this country.'[1] He asked 'why Parliament was to be broken up?' He demanded indignantly—'Can any sensible man, can any rational man, suppose that at this time of day, in this condition of the world, we are

[1] *Times*, September 27, 1871.

going to disintegrate the great capital institutions of this country for the purpose of making ourselves ridiculous in the sight of all mankind, and crippling any power we possess for bestowing benefits on the country to which we belong?'[1] On one occasion in 1877, and on another in 1880, we were consentient with our leader in repudiating as ' an impudent fiction ' any connection between the Liberal party and the Home Rule agitation,[2] and in repudiating any ' disposition to break down the authority of Parliament by fostering the Home Rule movement.'[3]

So far our leader and spokesman had confined himself to the political or constitutional objections founded on the magnitude of the changes involved in the breaking up of Parliament. But the moment his own new Government was formed in 1880, we were confronted by the facts which raised those moral objections that rest upon the lawless methods and the lawless aims of the Irish party. We began with the most virtuous intentions of governing Ireland without any exceptional executive powers. As I had the honour of being

[1] *Times*, September 27, 1871.   [2] *Times*, April 21, 1877.
[3] Speech, Juniper Green, March 21, 1880.

a member of that Government during the first twelve months of its existence, I share the right of others to insist upon it as a vital matter in the history of our time, that we were driven to ask for the coercive powers which Parliament gave to us, on clear proof and on the distinct allegation that they were absolutely needed to protect personal liberty, to repress crime, and violence, and anarchical designs, and not because we disapproved, however strongly, of Repeal or of Home Rule, or of any other measure, however mischievous, which might be promoted by Constitutional agitation. Our then leader was compelled to adopt this view of the situation, and he threw himself with all the energy of our common conviction into a corresponding attitude. He told Parliament in the solemn utterances of the Queen's Speech that ' an extended system of terror had been established in various parts of Ireland which had paralysed almost alike the exercise of private rights and the performance of civil duties.' Nothing short of such facts and convictions could have justified us in the measures we proposed. We asked and obtained the suspension of the Habeas Corpus Act, and an Arms Act. Mr.

Gladstone called them 'Protective measures.' He said in the Queen's Speech that these Acts were needed, 'not only for the vindication of order and public law, but likewise to secure on behalf of the Queen's subjects protection for life and property, and personal liberty of action.'

This is the period of the famous speeches at Leeds,[1] and at Knowsley,[2] which have been quoted *usque ad nauseam*, but which can never lose their value as witnesses of our unanimous consentience at the time, touching at least the facts with which we had to deal. I am not now speaking of any mere matter of opinion on the particular kind of executive weapon which we asked Parliament to place in our hands—the weapon, namely, of arbitrary arrest, or in other words, of imprisonment without trial. We all knew that the success of this weapon was open to doubt. We all knew that it was more or less experimental. But this has nothing to do with the facts, or with our estimate of the facts, touching the state of Ireland on which we were all consentient. Our leader was nothing but our common spokesman when he said at Knowsley that it was 'a contest

[1] *Times*, October 26, 1881.   [2] *Times*, October 28, 1881.

for the first and elementary principles upon which society is constituted,' that 'it was idle to talk of either law, or order, or liberty, or religion, or civilisation, if these gentlemen were to carry through the reckless and chaotic schemes that they had devised,' when he denounced 'these gentlemen' as 'wishing to march through rapine to disintegration and dismemberment of the Empire;' when finally, he declared that we were endeavouring 'to relieve the people of Ireland from the weight of a tyrannical yoke.'

I lay no stress on the extensive use made by Mr. Gladstone's Government of the powers confided to them. In this they were necessarily guided in the main by the local administration, represented in the Cabinet by the late Mr. Forster. Neither do I lay any stress on the capital made by our leader when, in the Guildhall, amidst the cheers of the 'classes,' and the ringing of the glasses, he announced the arrest of Mr. Parnell. Neither, on the other hand, do I lay any stress on the release of Mr. Parnell, and of others, after they had been incarcerated for six months, although Mr. Forster objected on the ground that they were released too unconditionally. There may have been excellent reasons for letting

'those gentlemen' out, without the least belief in
any change or repentance in them.   The prolonged
detention of men in prison without any trial,
and by the purely arbitrary act of the Executive,
might well be considered impolitic, especially if a
better and stronger substitute could be found.   Nobody was responsible for the personal belief into
which Mr. Gladstone was easily persuaded, that
'From   information   voluntarily   tendered,   these
gentlemen would find themselves in a condition
to range themselves on the side of what he should
call law and order and individual freedom in Ireland.'[1]   We shall probably never know the full
history of what was called—inaccurately no doubt,
and   perhaps   unjustly—the   Kilmainham   Treaty.
There   was   unquestionably   some   understanding,
although no definite bargain, about the passing
of an Act dealing with arrears of rent.   What is
certainly known, and what is fundamentally important, was that the Government of Mr. Gladstone
did not contemplate allowing the power of arbitrary arrest to expire without providing some new
and better weapon to take its place.   His own
belief in the reform of Mr. Parnell was purely per-

[1] *Hansard*, vol. 269, p. 124.

sonal. His resolution to ask Parliament for new legislation of another kind was not personal. In this he simply represented the common sense, not only of his own party, but of the country. His obscure language in the House of Commons on the release of Mr. Parnell and others, about his hopes of a change in their disposition, was instantly repudiated with anger by 'those gentlemen' themselves. They defied him to assert that they had done or said anything which could possibly imply the smallest pledge, direct or indirect, that they would change their course.

Then came the crash. Mr. Parnell was liberated on the 4th of May 1882. The Phœnix Park assassinations were perpetrated on the 6th. Mr. Gladstone's new Bill, which was to replace the power of arbitrary arrest, was introduced on the 11th. Yet the Minister took special pains to delare that his new Bill was '*not* founded on the recent outrages.' [1] The measure had been determined on before, as one demanded by the general condition of Ireland. Previous murders, he said, such as those of Mr. Herbert and Mrs. Smythe, had produced a great effect on the public mind. But he declared

[1] *Hansard*, vol. 269, p. 1119.

that not even these, nor any other outrages against the wealthier classes, had determined the Government in favour of the new Bill. What had determined them was mainly, and above all, ' the misery that had been carried far and wide among the body of the population.'[1] 'Outrage,' he insisted, 'had been committed in every form, even the most cruel and extreme.' In a country almost wholly agricultural, the ordinary transactions of life must, in a corresponding degree, be connected with agriculture, and between all the various classes dependent on it. Yet these were the very transactions in which the Minister declared that the administration of justice had become impossible. He asked indignantly ' whether the Government were to look with tolerance and indulgence upon the failure of the Jury system.'

Nothing short of continued proof of the anarchical methods and designs of the Irish party could have justified any Ministry in asking for such a measure as they proposed. It was indeed less purely arbitrary than the suspension of the Habeas Corpus Act. But for this very reason it was infinitely stronger. The object aimed at was not to

[1] *Hansard*, vol. 269, p. 1115.

suspend the ordinary law, but to strengthen it. It was to lift the administration of justice above the power of lawless terrorism. It gave power to try certain offences without the intervention of any jury—or rather it constituted a new jury out of the highest judges of the land—a proposition which assumed and implied a wide-spread demoralisation of the people, and a state of imminent danger to the foundations of Society. Such a measure as this, proposed by a responsible Government, is more eloquent than a hundred speeches.

In all other parts of the Bill it was of a corresponding character. It gave powers for the suppression of public meetings at the discretion of the Executive.[1] It gave powers equally stringent over the press.[2] It was the most extensive Coercion Act ever passed. Yet the Minister declared it to be merely a Bill of substitution for the arbitrary power of arrest. It was indeed this, but it was immensely more. A reform of the judicial apparatus was immeasurably better, because in its aim and object it was not arbitrary at all. Its aim and object was thoroughly constitutional. It was directed to reinforce the rights and liberties of the

[1] 45 and 46 Vict. ch. 25, sec. 10.   [2] *Ibid*. sec. B.

subject against lawless organisation—to redeem the administration of justice from the paralysis which these organisations had succeeded in effecting ; and to strengthen the Executive in its primary duty of enforcing law for the defence of the innocent, and for punishment of the guilty.

We were consentient with our leader, not only in these measures, but in the language and arguments which he used in their defence. He repudiated, as we now do, any attempt to claim toleration or lenity for lawlessness as any part of the true policy of conciliation. In reply to an Irish member who had called for this policy as identical with a policy of justice, Mr. Gladstone said — 'The article of justice satisfies me perfectly ; but I must remind the hon. member that it means justice to all and to every one. Unfortunately this includes the use of force for the punishment of evil-doers and the praise of all who do well.'[1]

Parliament gave to Mr. Gladstone's administration the great powers they asked, because it believed the facts which were alleged on the state of Ireland, and because it acknowledged those maxims of duty in respect to human government,

[1] *Hansard*, vol. 269, p. 1116.

which are of eternal truth and of universal obligation.

We had nothing to do then, and we have nothing to do now, with incidental passages in which our then leader, amongst other methods of opposing the Irish party, challenged them to produce their plan. There is no more effective way of resisting fundamental changes than by such challenges as these. He now dwells upon them as having had another meaning. It is just possible that they may have had some effect in encouraging the Irish party to persevere, in causing them to feel that the other words they heard were only bluster, and that the resisting substance in their front, despite its proud aspect, was, after all, only a wall of putty. It may be so : but we had nothing to do with that. Our consentience was with both sayings and doings which represented indisputable facts, and equally indisputable precepts, inseparably connected. One indisputable fact . was that the Irish party was aiming at anarchical objects, and the other was that they were working for these objects by lawlessness and tyranny. Both of these facts precluded discussion, and compelled our action.

Our former leader, in his *History of an Idea*, leaps from January 1882 to the fall of his Government in 1885.   Three notable years are thus dexterously left out of the account.   We need not wonder.   For his purposes they were indeed a blank.   But they are full of instruction for ours. They began with a boast on the part of the Prime Minister that 'this great conspiracy which, had it succeeded, would indeed have brought society to the very last of its resources, had been not only confronted but beaten.'[1]   Then had followed the release—then the murders—then the new Coercion Act—then three years of its firm administration by Lord Spencer.   In proportion as the powers given were duly exercised peace began to return in Ireland.   Men could breathe more freely.   The tyranny of conspirators was checked.   But there was no evidence of any change of temper or of designs on the part of Mr. Parnell and his party. Wherever they could speak freely, as always in America, or occasionally through the press in Ireland, and continually in the House of Commons, the same hostility was evinced towards the British Empire and towards the laws of civilisation.   Well

[1] *Hansard*, vol. 266, p. 182.

indeed did the Parnellite party in Parliament vindicate there, both in speech and in conduct, their angry disavowal of any promise, express or implied, that on their release they would be in a condition ' to range themselves on the side of law and order.'

It is most instructive to follow the speeches and the replies to questions made by the new Irish Secretary, Mr. Trevelyan, during the Sessions of 1882, 1883, and 1884. It was one long repeated task of contradicting falsehoods put in the form of interpellations, and of exposing direct incitements to disloyalty, or veiled—sometimes very thinly veiled—incitements to crime.[1] It is a sickening record ; and no change of tactics on the part of any Minister can in the slightest degree affect the evidence it affords of the conviction which was forced upon the mind of the Irish Secretary by personal knowledge, and by daily observation, of the elements we have to deal with in Irish disaffection.

During all this time our consentience was unbroken. It did not rest on mere opinions. It rested on the open and repeated acknowledgments

---

[1] See two remarkable speeches, February 22 and March 9, 1883. *Hansard*, vol. 276, pp. 726 and 1975.

of fundamental facts, and of primary duties and obligations.

Accordingly, when in 1885, the expiry of the Prevention of Crimes Act came to be close at hand, Mr. Gladstone's Government determined to renew all those parts of it which had been found to be most practically useful in securing the great object indicated in its title. Some of its provisions had never been used at all, such as the trial of criminals by a court of judges. But the means it allowed of strengthening juries, and of securing them and all witnesses from intimidation, which had been found to be efficient, were to be retained. Moreover, the Prime Minister had emphatically repudiated the name of coercion as justly applicable to such provisions.

There was nothing to affect our consentience from this date to the General Election of 1885. The interlude of a Conservative Government so weak in Parliamentary support that it could do nothing, and called to office at a moment when nothing could be done, was an interlude which could throw no new light upon the facts or upon our duty. The facts and the duty remained the same, whether, in trying to protect the Irish people from crime by trust in the ordinary law, the Conservative Cabinet were acting from sheer weakness and necessity; whether they were simply oversanguine; or whether they were resorting to a political manœuvre to secure the Irish vote. There was nothing necessarily dishonest in the attempt. At least it did not become us to treat it in this light. We had ourselves tried the same experiment when we came into office in 1879. On its failure we had confessed that failure, and had given up our experiment. It did not occur to any of us at the dissolution in 1885 that it would be consistent with our obligations to our country, and to its highest interests, that we should ascribe to the Conservative Government on this matter the worst motive, and that we should meet them in the spirit of the gamester who inwardly exclaims, 'Two can play at that trick. If you go in for an alliance with Mr. Parnell, so shall we, and we shall outbid you in that market.'

Dissentience did begin at this time. But it began underground, in the mind of our leader and not in ours. From the pages of his *History of an Idea* it is clear that he intended to educate the public mind, and prepare it for some great change, by words grave, serious, and perhaps even ominous, but carefully avoiding any definite indication of form or outline. Nothing was said which could be construed with even tolerable fairness into a foreshadowing of a separate Parliament and separate Executive for Ireland. The whole of the paragraphs which he quotes, as we read them now, in the light of subsequent events, were constructed on the plan of being susceptible of defensive quotation, afterwards, for anything he might do, and of not being susceptible of any definite interpretation, at the time, for anything he might intend. The reason for this was very frankly indicated in one of his Midlothian speeches. Mr. Parnell was at that moment holding himself up to auction between the two parties. He had invited Mr. Gladstone to show his hand, and to produce his plan. Mr. Gladstone ridiculed this demand, throwing the duty of proposing plans back upon the Irish members, and adding that by complying with such a challenge, ‘I should seriously damage any proposal which might have been hatched in my mind.’[1] This no doubt was perfectly true. But it means a great deal. ‘It

[1] Speech at Midcalder, November 17, 1885.

had then become morally certain,' as he tells us, 'that Ireland would, through a vast majority of her representatives, present a demand on the national sense,'[1] and most 'serious damage' indeed would have been done to the Liberal party if we had known that on this 'moral certainty' becoming a fact, he was prepared to 'break up the Imperial Parliament.'

It was not our business as public men, it was not the business of any subject of the Queen, to forecast the meaning of dark utterances like those, and to hold ourselves in readiness to accept any proposal that might be in the course of 'hatching.' Not one single sentence does our former leader quote as having been addressed to our reason on the merits of the Irish Question, with a view to show us that no such danger could arise from the breaking up of Parliament as had been impressed upon us by all the sayings and doings of our own and of former generations. Not one sentence does he quote as having been intended to show us that the Irish party had ceased, or would cease, to attack property and personal liberty. There was an absolute silence on this

---

[1] *History of an Idea*, p. 19.

matter which had been the very foundation of all our language and of all our measures. But this was not all. Two considerations were put before us with much emphasis—one was a warning that the demands of the Irish party went down to the 'roots of our civil and political constitution'; the other was that in order to deal with them it was above all things important that we should have a Liberal majority large enough to make us independent of the Irish vote.

This was a most natural doctrine to impress on the constituencies if—but only if—the Irish party contained dangerous elements against which it was necessary to guard. But the doctrine was not quite so natural if the Irish party were to be treated as altogether angelic—to be flattered, leant upon, cheered, and followed. Our education, therefore, was most imperfectly conducted when this was the lesson most urgently impressed upon us. It was quite according to the opinions to which we had been all consentient to be told that 'such a question could never be dealt with in a Parliament to the satisfaction of the country, unless there were present in it some party powerful enough to be independent of the Irish vote.'[1]

[1] Speech at Edinburgh, November 11, 1885.

Then followed events which will be memorable in the history of this country. The elections were completed. A Parliament was returned precisely of that character which Mr. Gladstone had indicated as incapable of dealing satisfactorily with the Irish problem. Mr. Parnell received that accession of strength which had been fully expected. On the other hand the Conservatives were not so swept off the board as to leave to the Liberals any large majority independent of the Irish vote. Independence being impossible, alliance might be tried. Accordingly, within a few weeks, an announcement was made through the National Press Agency, on December 16, 1885, that our leader had 'definitely adopted the policy of Home Rule for Ireland,' and that Lord Spencer would follow in his wake. On the 17th a similar intimation was published in the *Standard*, and at the same time was contradicted by Mr. Gladstone in terms so carefully limited and guarded that no doubt remained in the minds of any of us as to its substantial truth.

From this moment our consentience as to facts which we had all recognised as true, and in duties which we had all admitted to be binding, became of necessity dissentience with a leader who was evidently slipping away from both. This dissentience was his, not ours. We were running true. He was doubling on his own steps as well as on ours. He was, as we thought, in obvious alliance with those against whom we had fought in common. Every succeeding incident confirmed us in our old consentience by showing us what the new policy and the new alliance must involve.

When Parliament met in 1886, Mr. Parnell acted his part admirably. Mr. Gladstone now says[1] that the one new feature in the case which nobody could have foreseen was the speech on the first night of the Session of his former prisoner, and his new ally. If Mr. Parnell did not know the game he had to play he is not the man he is supposed to be. No direct communication was required. The situation was patent on the face of it. He had only to make a speech carefully modulated and restrained. He had been let out of prison without one word of promise or of compromise. He was now sure of welcome into a better lodging on even better terms. And so, if we read Mr. Parnell's speech in January 1886, on

[1] *History of an Idea*, p. 6-7.

which so much stress is now laid, we shall see
that just enough is said, both in tone and substance, to smooth the approaches of his former
opponent, without saying one word that pledged
him to any abandonment of his old aims or of
his old methods.

Then came still more astonishing events. The
Conservative Government was turned out by the
use of Mr. Jesse Collings as a pawn. A new
Cabinet was formed, and our former leader was
compelled to open his mind a little wider to his
old associates. Enough had been said to necessi-
tate explicit questions, and some approach at least
to explicit answers. These seem to have been
postponed as long as possible. But the proposal
which had been 'hatching' broke the shell at last.
The result was an immediate revolt on the part
of every one of the more independent minds which
had formerly served under the same leader. Lord
Hartington, Mr. Bright, Mr. Chamberlain, Mr.
Goschen, Sir George Trevelyan, were a group of
men representing Liberal opinion as typically, in
some respects more typically, than Mr. Gladstone
himself. One new man of undoubtedly independent mind, and of considerable literary eminence,

Mr. John Morley, was included in the group which seceded with Mr. Gladstone into the alliance with Mr. Parnell.

Then followed the most wonderful phenomenon of all. This group of men—all of them highly respectable, and one of them illustrious—sat down to evolve out of their own inner consciousness, and in a few weeks, a brand-new British Constitution. A Conservative Cabinet had once been compelled, under great pressure, to devise a Reform Bill in ten minutes. It was called the 'Ten Minutes Bill.' But this was child's play to the undertaking of that cluster of politicians who met in Downing Street in February 1886, and promised that early in April they would produce a scheme, 'going down to the very roots and foundations of our whole civil and political constitution,' which would provide an adequate substitute for a broken Parliament and a disunited kingdom.

On this subject it is our duty to speak freely. There are some things in this world which are greater even than the greatest man—more binding on us than loyalty to the oldest leader—and which ought to be dearer to us than even the dearest friend. One of these things is that which we call the Constitution of our country. This is not— let it be emphatically repeated—any mere law. It is not even any code. Still less is it any mere organic statute. Neither is it any system of mechanical devices for checking and counter-balancing the different tendencies of different classes of men. 'The roots and foundations of our whole civil and political constitution' are the roots and foundations of all our rights, of all our duties and obligations, and of all our understand-ings both of public and of private virtue. In our country these have been shaped and formed and sanctioned by the work of centuries, and have been embodied in institutions which have grown, and have never been invented. It is no dis-paragement to any man to say that we deny his competence to go down to these roots, and to cut, prune, and relay them as he pleases, without danger to our dearest interests. A man may be very illustrious indeed without being fit for this. Prob-ably the most brilliant achievement of Mr. Glad-stone was his great Budget, or scheme of financial adjustment, in 1853. I had the honour of being one of his colleagues in that Cabinet, and I know,

as few perhaps know or recollect now, the difficulties he had to overcome. I shall never forget
the impression made upon us all by the originality
of conception, the courage, resource, knowledge,
dexterity of treatment, and breadth of view,
through which alone that scheme secured its
splendid success in Parliament. But no scheme
of readjusted taxation is in the least degree comparable in magnitude, or in kind, to a scheme
which is to break up the Imperial Parliament,
and reconstitute the British Constitution. Again,
Mr. Gladstone's measure disestablishing the Irish
Church was justly admired as an excellent bit of
work. But here, also, the difficulty was essentially
financial — the system of commutation and the
principle on which property was to be divided.
There was no society to be pulled to pieces, and
to be set up again on a new plan, and inspired
with new ideas. The society to be dealt with was
the Christian Church. He had nothing to do but
to let it alone. There was nothing to be done
in the way of reconstruction there.

So far, then, as skill or experience are concerned
in the duty of devising a new political constitution,
Mr. Gladstone was as purely a ' 'prentice hand '

as any other Englishman, or Scotchman, or Irishman, in any of the three kingdoms.

But there is more to be said than this against any facile acquiescence in such a work as was actually undertaken. Our Parliamentary Government, especially as developed in recent times, puts an enormous premium on the powers of speech. Mr. Gladstone, more perhaps than any public man who has ever occupied a like position, uses, and depends upon this power. Constantly, and as by a natural instinct, he declines to allow any opinion he has ever expressed to be quoted or described in words other than his own. His great parliamentary expositions bristle with ingenuities of statement. Subtle distinctions, and sometimes equally subtle confoundings of distinction, are continually involved when they are entirely unperceived by those who hear him. Dexterous appeals to different sentiments and to sections of opinion, equally refined and effective, are parts of his apparatus in the handling of the great popular assembly in which he has been so long predominant. Now this is, perhaps, of all training the most dangerous in the making of Constitutions. It leads men to be the victims of their own eloquence

—firm believers in the power and virtue of mere words and phrases. For the purpose of swaying popular assemblies at the moment, these are indeed invaluable; and of course they may be yoked to service in a good cause as well as in a bad one. But of all the sources of danger and of fatal error which can beset a statesman who assumes to frame an organic statute for the government of mankind, perhaps this volubility in phrases, and this trust in them, is the most pestilent, because the most prolific.

Accordingly, the new British Constitution, which he now expressly declares he meant to be in principle equally applicable, not only to Ireland, but to Scotland and to Wales,[1] and which he 'hatched' with his little ring and residuum of colleagues in the course of sixty-six days, was perhaps the most extraordinary proposal ever submitted to an assembly of men who had been brought up in, and were familiar with, an ancient and time-honoured political system. It was ingenious; but its ingenuity was largely verbal. It had a principle and an aim underlying it; but that principle and aim was not only unavowed, but much clever phraseology was employed to disguise or conceal

[1] *History of an Idea*, p. 5; *Lessons of the Elections*, p. 36, etc.

it. The aim was to get rid of an obstructive element in the House of Commons by the elimination of the Irish members. In this view, and on this principle, a very great deal can be said in its favour. It was a proposal infinitely better than any mere mendings of it which have been since demanded, and since apparently allowed. The so-called 'concessions' have been all for the worse, because they were elements wholly alien to its original conception, inconsistent with its principle, and inconsistent with common sense. The granting of them, if indeed this was really intended, was the final and most conclusive proof of the levity and the rashness with which the very nerve-centres and ganglions of our political organisation cut, and hacked, and handled, by the quack doctors who assume to mend it.

It has sometimes amused me to speculate on the reception with which Mr. Gladstone would have greeted his own proposals of the 8th of April 1886, if they had been made by another man and in the interests of another party! How he would have rushed at them, stamped upon them, and torn them into shreds and tatters! It does indeed seem like a joke or a dream when we re-

D

member what some of the salient features of those
proposals were, the manner of their proposal, and
the manner in which they have been since handled
by their own parents.   One great characteristic
stares us in the face.   Ireland was encouraged and
stimulated to think of herself as a separate
nationality in the most exaggerated terms—terms
wholly at variance with history, whether it be the
history of race or of institutions.   And all this
inflated language ended in the proposal to reduce
Ireland to the condition of a tributary province,
with no share whatever in Imperial concerns.
The leader of the Liberal party was exhibited
devising a new Constitution on the complete and
systematic severance of representation and taxation.   Nor were the Irish to get in exchange anything approaching to those powers of Home Rule
which are naturally associated with the idea of
a separate nationality such as they were not only
allowed, but were incited, to assert.   The garrison
of Ireland was to be of those who were stigmatised
as foreigners.   She was not even to be allowed to
regulate her own taxation in the great items of
Customs and Excise.   Her tribute to the Imperial
Exchequer was to be fixed for a long period of

years.   Further contributions might be asked in
the case of foreign war—war in the policy of
which the Irish people could have no voice, but
still war which might be intimated to the
separate Irish Parliament by a gracious communication from the Throne.

All this was recommended or defended on the
alleged success of foreign and colonial institutions
—not one of which bears the faintest likeness to
the new constitution proposed for Ireland.   There
is not one of our Colonies which would not repudiate such a constitution as worthy only of the
days of George Grenville and of Charles Towns-
hend.   There is not one of the provinces of which
the great colony of Canada is composed, for example, which, in its relations even with the Central
Legislature or Dominion Parliament, would tolerate
such a constitution for a moment.   The whole
device was essentially incapable of solving the
problem, if it was imperative to attempt such a
problem at all.   It showed no appreciation of the
forces which must be evoked by the setting up
of a separate Parliament, with loud - mouthed en-
couragements to think and to boast of itself as
representing a separate nationality.   It was like a

new form of steam-engine, built up in all its tubes, boilers, cylinders, and condensers, of some such material as papier-maché, coloured, glazed, and painted with the flowers of rhetoric, but without any estimate of the tremendous pressures exerted by the expansive powers of steam.

In saying this I am not saying that Mr. Gladstone had no good reason for his proposal to eliminate the Irish members from the Imperial Parliament. He had two most excellent reasons, one of which he gave, and on the other of which he was silent. He was silent on the fact that the Irish members had succeeded in making themselves intolerable. They were not only disloyal to the Empire, but they were specially and immediately disloyal to the great assembly in which they sat. They had lowered its character, impeded its business, and were shaking its authority. If such conduct and dispositions were really to be permanent, there could be no resource except to do without them. Irishmen have been, and ought to be again, an ornament to that House. The natural genius of the people eminently adapts them to shine in popular assemblies. But no assembly can live or work with a whole group of members who are disloyal to it, who use its forms to discredit it, and who convert its ancient privileges, which were intended to secure its liberty, into weapons directed to the destruction of its life. This was the real cause of, although not the avowed reason for, the proposal of Mr. Gladstone.

But the reason which he did assign was an excellent reason too, because closely connected with the other. If Ireland was to have a separate Parliament, her members could not be allowed to rule Great Britain as well as their own country. This would be intolerable indeed. In objecting to this our former leader was consentient with us and with himself. This was the very objection upon which for ten years he had challenged his opponents to produce an intelligible plan. So early as 1874 he had denounced with ridicule 'the proposal of the Irish leader,' by defining it thus :—
'That plan is this—that exclusively Irish affairs are to be judged in Ireland, and then that the Irish members are to come to the Imperial Parliament and to judge as they may think fit of the general affairs of the Empire, and also of affairs exclusively English and Scotch.'[1] On the

---

[1] *History of an Idea*, pp. 14-15.

Irish leader shouting 'No!' Mr. Gladstone turned upon him—'It is all very well for gentlemen to cry "No" when the blot has been hit.' And he now admits that his own special objection ever since has been to any 'proposal that Irishmen should deal exclusively with their own affairs, and also jointly with ours.'[1]

So far Mr. Gladstone was perfectly right. But he was right only on one assumption, namely, that the breaking up of our Imperial Parliament is a work that must be done. To those who do not admit that assumption, the proposal to eliminate the Irish members, and to reduce Ireland to a tributary province, whilst simultaneously her people are incited to claim a separate nationality, is a proposal which only confirms our insuperable objections to the whole scheme as incongruous and impossible. And so, again, we do not deny the force of another subsidiary argument of Mr. Gladstone, namely this, that it passes the wit of man so to separate between Irish and Imperial affairs as to keep the Irish members in the Parliament at Westminster, and yet prevent them from that undue interference with our affairs

---

[1] *History of an Idea*, p. 15.

which would be intolerable when they have a separate Parliament of their own. We admit the force of this argument, and we are glad that in this matter at least our little group of political architects did feel, at least for a time, some fraction of the difficulties to be encountered in rebuilding the British Constitution. But our admission of this argument only confirms again, by a most effective illustration, the chaotic results of the presumptuous attempt which we are resisting.

We are confirmed, too, in the stand we have made, and in the resistance which we continue to offer, by the exhibition which these architects have made of themselves on this very matter in the later stages of our contest. Mr. Gladstone himself began, almost at once, the exhibition of instability and irresolution which are the sure symptoms of rash and heedless counsels. Nothing could be more emphatic than his language on the famous 8th of April in the unfolding of his scheme. 'There cannot,' he said, 'be a domestic Legislature in Ireland dealing with Irish affairs, and Irish peers and Irish representatives sitting in Parliament at Westminster to take part in English and

Scotch affairs.' He was inclined to believe that this 'would be universally admitted.' Neither could we draw a distinction between affairs which are Imperial and affairs which are not Imperial so as to make it 'practicable for Irish representatives to come here for the settlement, not of English and Scotch, but of Imperial affairs.' He had 'thought much, reasoned much, and inquired much, with regard to that distinction.' We had hoped it might be possible to draw it. But he 'had arrived at the conclusion that it cannot be drawn.' He 'believed it passes the wit of man to do so.'

Five days later the sails of this good ship were seen to be shaking in the wind. The helmsman was unsteady. On April 13 Mr. Gladstone referred to the problem as 'one which British statesmanship might be found adequate to solve.' He would not 'close the door against any considerations of this kind.' On the 1st of May he told the Midlothian electors that this was a mere detail. By the 10th of May the vessel of our state was fairly on the tack. The Prime Minister would provide in Committee that 'when a proposal is made to alter the taxation in respect of customs and excise, Irish members shall have an opportunity of appearing in this House to take a share in the transaction of that business.'[1] Nor was this all. The subject involved no vital principle, 'nor had the Government aimed at any binding decision.'

This has been the cue ever since. The whole Anglo-Parnellite alliance has been cautious, because disunited, on the subject. They have pretended to treat this question of the inclusion or exclusion of the Irish Members in the Imperial Parliament as a question of detail. Yet nothing can be more clear than that almost everything turns and depends upon it. If the Irish Members are to be kept as, and where, they are, then their so-called separate Parliament can be nothing but some provincial body possessing little more than the powers of a great Town Council or a great County Board. This is absolutely inconsistent with the whole tone and language of the demand made by the Parnellite party, and seconded with fervour by their new Anglican ally. If, on the other hand, the Irish Members, being kept as they are in numbers, are to be restrained and limited as

---

[1] *Speeches on the Irish Question*, 1886, p. 131.

regards the subjects on which they are to be allowed to vote, then the whole scheme must be reconstructed from top to bottom, and a task must be undertaken which Mr. Gladstone had declared to be beyond the wit of man. If, again, as a third alternative, Ireland is to be represented at Westminster by a limited number of representatives sent as a delegation from its own separate Parliament, or from its separate constituencies—then we are landed in a Federal Constitution which is absolutely different in its nature from the proposal actually made, and as widely different from the ancient Constitution of the United Kingdoms.

Is it possible to retain any respect for the political judgment and knowledge of a group of men who play fast and loose with us upon such a subject as this—and who, manifestly, are not agreed among themselves on the fundamental principles on which the new British Constitution is to be framed ? One prominent member of the party has lately spoken with ridicule and contempt of the very notion that the Irish Members can be retained in the Imperial Parliament after they have been established in a separate Parliament of their own, and asks whether they are to be summoned like waiters by the ringing of a bell when some question arises on which they are allowed to vote.[1] Another member of the party, again, treats this kind of difficulty as a mere invention of the enemy, and intimates that the problem which passes the wit of Mr. Gladstone is quite easily to be solved by the genius of Mr. Childers.

Such exhibitions as these cut deeply into any trace of confidence which might have been left in the knowledge and capacity of those who assume to guide us through a tremendous experiment. But there are other facts affecting quite as deeply our trust in them touching matters which, to us, are matters of honour and of conscience. For many years we have been consentient with them in recognising as a fact that the Irish party did not seem to be bound by the accepted doctrines of civilised societies in respect to property and personal freedom in the transactions of ordinary life. This was the only meaning and the only defence of such speeches as those delivered by our then Leader in 1882. It was the only meaning and the only justification of the Bills he then brought in for the repression of crime and the protection of liberty—of the repeated testimony he

[1] Earl of Rosebery.

bore to the urgent necessity which demanded them
—and of the strong action which, during three
years, he took in the exercise of their powers. It
was in continuous support and illustration of this
fact, and of the terrible evidence which proved its
truth, that Sir George Trevelyan and his successor
in the Irish Office, were engaged night after night
in the House of Commons, down to the very close
of Mr. Gladstone's Government in 1885, in exposing the tyrannies and crimes of the Irish Land
League, and in exposing also the close connection
between the political action of Irish Members
and the more conspicuous outbursts of crime.

PART II.

THE NEW PAPER CONSTITUTION:
HOW IT WAS SCHEMED
AND DROPPED.

—•—

IT was our absolute duty to remember all the preceding facts when the same Ministers came to present us with a new Constitution breaking up the Imperial Parliament, and setting up a separate Parliament and Executive for Ireland. It is always open to all men to change their opinions. But it is not open to any man to suppress facts when he undertakes a public duty on which these facts have a direct and immediate bearing. We looked, therefore, for some features in the new Constitution which might recognise the special facts so long acknowledged and so long proved by indisputable evidence.

We found one such feature of it in the Land Bill. The danger to property was acknowledged there. Nothing else could justify or account for so formidable a proposal. The owners of land in Ireland — ranging from those who had bought property quite recently, under the direct guarantee and authority of Courts appointed for the purpose, up to families which have been settled in Ireland for seven hundred years, and have been 'more Irish than the Irish'—all these were offered the option of selling their property and clearing out of their native country if they were afraid to live in it under the new Constitution. I am not undervaluing this offer. It was at least an honest one to make; but it involved a tremendous confession. It was absolutely demanded by honour if—but only if—all property in Ireland was to be handed over to a Government which could not be trusted to respect it. There are some political proposals which speak for themselves. Their meaning cannot be misunderstood. No forms of language, more ingenious than ingenuous, on the part of a Minister in proposing them can affect their significance. And this proposal was one of these. I fully admit that it was hardly and even unjustly treated; but the man who treated it most unjustly was the Minister himself. Nothing could carry such a measure except the strongest sentiment of duty and of honour, and nothing could establish a case of duty and of honour except a frank confession that the new British Constitution was to hand over all the holders of property in Ireland to a Government animated by the morality of the Land League. But this was exactly what it did not suit the rest of the Minister's plan that he should acknowledge too distinctly.

To this, and to another circumstance, we doubtless owed the extraordinary speech which ushered in the proposal. There was an interval of eight days between the introduction of the new Irish Government Bill and that of the Irish Land Purchase Bill.[1] This interval had been long enough to show that Irish landowners generally were not disposed to be 'bought out '—to desert their country, or to live on in their old houses reduced to villas, and connected with nothing but some covers, some pleasure-grounds, and a garden. They could not be brought to believe so suddenly that this was really the only alternative left to their choice. The homes they loved and had lived in for genera-

---

[1] April 8th to April 16th.

E

tions, the property they had inherited, and all the associations connected with them, they clung to still. Every consideration of justice and of generosity demanded that this feeling should be recognised and respected. It was at least natural, if indeed not actually meritorious. The obvious policy of any Minister, too, if he had a single eye to the success of his proposal, was to argue in the same spirit—to point out how much had been done to deprive ownership of land in Ireland of all that could operate hardly on the tenant class, and what a high and honourable obligation lay on Parliament to protect owners in the enjoyment of what remained. Instead of this, the speech of the Minister was little more than one long raking up of all old sores against Irish landowners, just as if every alleged grievance were still as operative as ever—just as if he himself had never introduced and carried any Land Bill, completely removing them, whatever else it did. Formally indeed, and in words, the proposal was founded on 'serious convictions both of honour and of duty;'[1] but no argument was used to make clear wherein that obligation consisted, or whence it

---

[1] *Speeches on the Irish Question*, 1886, p. 108.

flowed—except, indeed, the offensive argument that the Imperial Legislature was *particeps criminis* in all the alleged evils of Irish landed property, and that Irish landowners were to be regarded as our 'garrison' in a foreign country.[1] Yet some better argument than this was imperatively demanded to overcome the natural and inevitable objections which rose up from many sides against a proposal so large in itself and so revolutionary in the confessions it involved. If the speech had been specially directed to rouse a spirit hostile to the measure, instead of favourable to it, no arguments more ingenious could have been devised. And in addition to this tendency of the speech as regards its whole texture and direction, Irish members connected with property could not help feeling that the speech was delivered in a tone of great bitterness against those who refused to sacrifice their country and their homes.

Then there was another feature in the handling of this matter, against which we protest firmly, as involving assumptions of power and of right on the part of political leaders, in which it would be absolutely inconsistent with our honour to have any

[1] *Speeches on the Irish Question,* 1886, p. 83.

share. I refer to the passage in an address to the electors of Midlothian, issued May 1, 1886, in which the owners of property in Ireland were warned that 'the sands were running in the hour-glass.'[1] Prophecy may be legitimate to political leaders, but not prophecy of the kind which involves a threat. A mountaineer may warn a traveller in the valley beneath him that rocks or avalanches are on the move. But if that mountaineer is a man who stands with cartridges and levers in his hands to loosen the stones and bring down the snow, then his prophecy becomes a threat. This is and must be the position of a political leader who tells the owners of property that unless they do something that he bids them they will be ruined and despoiled.

Some of us were consentient with Mr. Gladstone in proposing, and we are all now in the position of having acquiesced with him in carrying, the most fundamental changes in landed property of Ireland. He did, indeed, just passingly allude to these measures in his speech ;[2] but he alluded to them as a subject on which he would not dwell, as 'it was beside his argument.' That indeed was true. It was beside his particular argument. But it was

[1] *Speeches on the Irish Question*, 1886, p. 173.   [2] *Ibid.* p. 88.

not beside the question to which that argument applied. It was strictly relevant to that question, and it condemned the relevancy of the arguments he did employ, and the justice of the reproaches he levelled at the victims of his new policy.

Nothing could induce us to be parties to the use of language implying such threats under the guise of prophecies. We don't assume the right to accuse others of any conscious violation of justice or of duty. But we are firm in declaring that for ourselves, and in our own consciences, we never could be parties to the use of such language, or to the policy which it implies. We deem it contrary to our duty to propose or to vote for any constitution which exposes private persons to plunder and the loss of all individual freedom, with no other escape than the acceptance of exile and of commutation in money. All the dexterities of language by which the nakedness of such a proposal was disguised are devices with which we could not be associated even in the smallest measure.

But if we protest against the manner in which this proposal was made, we protest, if possible, even more strongly against the manner in which it was withdrawn. If it was a proposal once, or ever, made 'under serious convictions both of honour and of "duty,"'[1] it must remain an obligation in spite of any amount of reluctance or opposition on the part either of those to whom the offer was made, or on the part of Parliament. There is always one simple and obvious alternative open to a leader and to a party who make a proposal of this acknowledged character and find themselves unable to carry it. They may relinquish a scheme which is thus deprived of a condition essential to its justice and to its honourable character ; or they may themselves cease to strive for office, or for the retention of office, when it can no longer be held except on the terms of abandoning such an obligation. But neither of these courses was the one actually taken. In making the proposal words were used which seemed to proclaim that it was an inseparable part of the whole scheme. But this meaning was hedged by other words which reserved an outlet of retreat. The inseparability was cautiously declared to be ' in our own minds, and for the existing juncture.'[2] Such, at least, is the account given of it since.

[1] *Speeches on the Irish Question*, p. 108.
[2] *Lessons of the Elections*, p. 44.

But this is no inseparability at all. Such words conveyed no pledge whatever; and accordingly the moment it became clear that Irishmen such as the Fitzgeralds, and the Butlers, and the Hamiltons, and a thousand others, were loyal to the Union, and were not prepared to abandon their ancient position in their native country, the proposal of purchase was ostentatiously withdrawn, as if with the exultation of men to whom an opportunity has been happily opened of shaking themselves free from an acknowledged but inconvenient obligation. It is now declared to have been 'swept ruthlessly off the field of present action.' 'The twinship' of the two Bills is denounced as 'having been for the time disastrous to the hopes of Ireland,' which means disastrous to the hopes of the Parnellite alliance. Therefore it is added emphatically that this twinship 'exists no longer.'

But a new bargain is advertised. The twinship of the two Bills being dissolved the author of them is free to make another twinship, more close and intimate—the twinship, namely, between his own party and the party of Mr. Parnell. Let Home Rule be granted without any such clog on its operations. Let the owners of property who have opposed

the Purchase Bill look out in future for themselves.
It will, Mr. Gladstone confesses, need all their
vigilance for the purpose of preventing the adoption of schemes of Land Purchase founded on principles very different from, and indeed opposite to,
those of the Bill lately consigned to the limbo of
abortions.[1]

What can this mean? Who are the men from
whom this danger is to come? Is it from the
proposed separate Parliament in Ireland? Then
are we to understand it to be now confessed that
property in Ireland is to be left to the doctrine
of spoliation? And how is this warning threat
to be reconciled with the declaration that the safe-
guards for minorities which had been proposed were
not provided in consequence of any mistrust entertained by Mr. Gladstone, but only 'in consequence
of mistrust entertained by others'? What are we
to believe? Is there, or is there not, just cause for
apprehension to the owners of property if they be
left to be dealt with by a separate Irish Parliament?
Is it true, or is it not true, that danger to them
would be so real that our honour and our obligation demanded the most onerous, the most unusual,

---

[1] *Lessons of the Elections*, p. 46.

precautions? Or is it true, on the contrary, that all such precautions were merely ' contributions to disarm honest, though unfounded jealousies '? Or, lastly, is it true that one at least of these unfortunate minorities is only too probably to be exposed to the obscurely worded but darkly foreboded dangers shadowed forth in this angry passage?

We dare not follow any leader who leads us thus. We dare not dissever the duty of devising special measures for protecting individual freedom and property, and all the privileges of British subjects, when we are devising other measures which, as we know and confess, will expose them to special dangers. We have a right to know what is meant by all this language of menace against men whom, along with all other men, it is the absolute duty of responsible statesmen to protect in all their just and legal interests; and we ask whether it has indeed become part of the creed of the reorganised Liberal party, that when any class of men exercises its right to judge and act freely on great constitutional proposals they are to be thus threatened, and, if possible, bullied into acquiescence?

Then there is another feature of the conduct

and language of the new Parnellite alliance on
this subject, which is indeed less offensive, but is
very little more worthy of respect. They do not
openly deny, or pretend to deny, that an Irish
Home Rule Parliament would so act, or would
probably so act, as to endanger property and
attack the fundamental principles on which it
rests. Yet they don't like—it does not suit their
game to say so openly. They fall back upon the
device of representing the whole land question as
one too heavy to be thrown upon the shoulders
of the new Irish Parliament. In pure charity and
kindness we ought to take it off their hands
before we start them on their way. This is one
of the methods of expression adopted in Mr.
Gladstone's first speeches on the subject, and it
is one by which Lord Spencer has been frequently
of late escaping from inconvenient avowals. But
here again we cannot ourselves consent to employ
these evasions. If the new. Irish Parliament cannot be trusted to deal with this subject, it must
be because they are not expected to be bound by
the ordinary laws of civilised society. And if this
be true of this particular subject, what confidence
can we have that it may not be equally true of

their probable attitude on many other subjects? Moreover, as agrarian questions are the main questions affecting Irish society in all its phases, what guarantee can be given — what reasonable hope can be held out to us—that the new Irish nationality, with its new Parliament and its new Executive, will acquiesce—except for some purpose of their own, and for the moment—in its exclusion from powers of 'Home Rule' over that very branch of legislation which interests and excites them most?

Not only, therefore, the proposal of the Land Purchase Bill, but all the circumstances attending it, and especially the language attending its withdrawal, prove to demonstration that our former leaders who undertook to draw up a new British Constitution in sixty-six days have not only completely broken down in the attempt, but that they have exhibited a character in respect to the most solemn public obligations, which must inspire us with profound distrust.

Before the division on the second reading had been taken, and still more before the subsequent appeal to the constituencies, more and more of the lumber of the new constitution had to be thrown overboard. Not even the great personal influence of our former leader could have secured even a tolerable minority unless he had given it to be clearly understood that the whole scheme was open to a complete recast. In spite of this practical abandonment of everything definite in the proposal, he was defeated by a considerable majority, and when he and his supporters went to the country there seemed to be a positive competition which of them should repudiate most loudly being bound to either of the two Bills, or to any part of them.

Such a scene has never before been presented in our political history. The Liberal party was reduced to a set of men who were to follow a leader with nothing in his mouth but an empty phrase—'The Irish people were to have the management of exclusively Irish affairs.' Nothing more definite was vouchsafed. The formula had certain variations—some of them ingenious—but most of them purely verbal, and none of them throwing the least light on the practical measures to which they pointed. In the *History of an Idea* we may count some twelve or fourteen editions or variations of this phrase. We were expected not to ask the simplest questions—not to test the meaning of the words dinned into our ears, or repeated by our lips. Is safety to life, liberty, and property in Ireland an 'exclusively Irish affair'? Is the right of every Irishman—labourer or tradesman—to work for whom he likes, an 'exclusively Irish affair'? Is the right of every Irish shopkeeper to sell to all who will give him custom an exclusively Irish affair? Is the right of every Irishman to be honest if he pleases in paying his just debts an 'exclusively Irish affair'? May a poor Irishman hire a little farm if he likes for the support of his family without fear of being cruelly murdered—is this also an affair 'exclusively Irish'? Is all Imperial duty and responsibility in the enforcement of human rights and obligations in Ireland to be considered an 'exclusively Irish affair'?

These are a few, and a few only, of the questions which must be answered before we can put any intelligible meaning on the windy phrases under which we are summoned to consent to the breaking up of our Parliamentary Constitution, and to the unknown and undefined inventions by which it is to be replaced.

Moreover, in seeking to probe these questions to the bottom—as it is our absolute duty to do—there is one consideration which we cannot forget. The Irish members of the Parnellite party had agreed to the plan by which they were to be excluded from the Imperial Parliament and all its concerns, and were to be relegated to a subordinate Parliament in Ireland, limited to affairs 'exclusively Irish.' They had thus 'sold their country,' in a sense which can never be applied even by the most rabid opponent of Mr. Pitt's Union—to the Irish members who voted for that measure in 1800. It cannot be asserted that they divorced their country from Imperial concerns. On the contrary, for them at least, it must be owned that if they gave up something for Ireland as regarded a separate Legislature, they gained for Ireland, on the other hand, and for the first time, the splendid privilege of an equal proportionate share in the government and legislation of the noblest Empire in the world. But these Parnellite members were sacrificing that position after it had been attained ; they were sinking their country again to a position distinctly lower, subordinate, and tributary. And for what? What was the price they were to get for this

great surrender ?   Nothing was said, but much
might be suspected.   Was it the opportunity for
that which Mr. Gladstone had himself denounced
as plunder ?   What proof had he given, or even
suggested, that there was any fundamental change
in the aims and objects of the Irish party ?   Did
he not himself point out, in the very speech in
which he expounded his new plan, that crime was
rife in Ireland, and the law was not maintained ?
The pretext that this arose from the ' foreign
character' of the law, was a pretext which suggested changes in that law to suit the ideas which,
by contrast, might be native.   And what were
these ?   The ideas of the Land League ?   Let the
ghastly spectacle reply of that old man in the
wilds of Kerry, who was lately nursing a small
farm for his daughter's husband, and who for this
crime has been murdered in the most cruel and
brutal manner — his limb shattered by repeated
shots, left in agony where neither doctor could
reach him to relieve his body, nor priest have
access to soothe his soul, until death put an
end to his misery with his life.   Such deeds
as these are deeds that have a significance far
beyond what is called ' ordinary crime.'   Irishmen

are accustomed to boast sometimes that in Ireland 'ordinary crime' is small.   But the crime which is common is precisely that which affects the character of large portions of the people, because of its indicating either a wide prevalence of popular sympathy, or else a wide submission to tyranny and terror.   But both of these are precisely the conditions which sound the most warning of all notes against the safety of intrusting to the rulers in such a community the lives, liberty, and property of their fellow-subjects.

And this brings me to one feature in Mr. Gladstone's course which may well inspire us with special distrust.   We have seen that when he proposed his own Prevention of Crimes Bill he emphatically declared that it was less the murders and outrages perpetrated on the wealthier classes than the sufferings of the humble and the poor under the tyranny of the Land League, which had induced him and his colleagues to apply for special legislation.   This description of the facts was true, whatever we may think of the value and the virtue of the distinction drawn.   And this fact continued to be true in 1886, as it continues to be true at the present moment.   Nothing in the conduct and

language of the Anglo-Parnellites is more unjustifiable than the new pretence that Irish crime
is chiefly connected with exorbitant rents and unjust evictions. They know perfectly well that
crime is most rife against and amongst the poor,
as a means of enforcing the tryanny of the League
upon thousands who would gladly escape from it
if they could or dared. They know perfectly well
that in a large part of Ireland the organisation
is so complete that there is no sort of independence
among the mass of the people. They know that
this tyranny enters into the field of politics, and
is specially directed to securing an exclusive support to the leader of the organisation. Yet it is
under these conditions that our former leader has
called on us to break up the Parliament of the
United Kingdom, on the plea that Ireland as a
nation has finally and unequivocally declared that
she seeks Home Rule by an overwhelming majority
of her representatives.

On general grounds, and without circumstances
very special, we might fairly demur to accepting
such a necessity as that of rebuilding the British
Constitution on the strength of sudden general
elections on a new franchise, and the result of which

F

is, after all, far from unanimous. Fundamental changes going, by admission, down to the very roots of the Constitution, both civil and political, are not changes which can be safely determined by plebiscites. Probably the worst Government which has ever been set up in modern Europe—that of Napoleon III.—was founded on a plebiscite which I believe was perfectly genuine, and quite as independent as any such vote can be said to be. The impulses under which the masses may be got to vote away the liberties of others, and their own, are impulses as numerous as they are unsafe. But in this particular case of Ireland there are a multitude of very special circumstances which detract from the value and significance of the popular vote. In the first place, a very large part of the voters are extremely ignorant, and had only just been admitted to the franchise. The exercise of such a power for the first time by a people wholly unaccustomed to, and unfitted for, deliberate thought upon the deepest questions affecting Society, must be an exercise peculiarly liable to error. In no country in the world, perhaps, certainly in none of the old countries of Europe, would it be reasonably safe to be guided by such a vote in such matters. But in

Ireland we know as a fact that this class is now widely under terror—dominated by secret societies which visit all who are honest and independent with violence, outrage, and persecution. We know that a very large percentage were so ignorant that they even belong to the class formally declaring themselves to be 'illiterate,' and unable to sign their names. We know that the votes of all these men were under the direct control of agents of the Land League, who attended at the polls to keep them in obedience.

Under such conditions, even if the vote had been much larger and much more unanimous than it was, it would be absurd in any rational statesman to quote it or describe it as a deliberate decision of the people of Ireland, on the strength of which we are to unsay all that we have been saying touching questions of duty and morality, or to enter into a conspiracy of silence on facts which we had all been quoting as equally indisputable and important. Yet this is the course taken by the Anglo-Parnellites. There is something specially suspicious in the vehemence with which Mr. Gladstone, from the first moment that the elections were over, began to reiterate that Ireland had declared its mind in a

manner that could not and ought not to be even for
for a moment questioned.   Politicians are very apt
to be thus specially dogmatic and enthusiastic on
some point which their inner conscience tells them
is dangerously weak.   It is instructive to observe
the very different spirit in which Mr. Gladstone has
treated the verdict of the people of Great Britain
at the polls.   He falls upon that verdict fiercely
with all the resources of his arithmetical faculty,
and absolutely refuses to accept it as justifying even
a momentary suspension of his efforts to reverse it.
There is nothing even tolerable—far less anything
so sacred as to be above criticism—in the verdict of
the people of Great Britain.   But the Irish populace
—to a large extent poor, ignorant, league-ridden,
cowed, and systematically intimidated—are to be
taken at their first word, and without a murmur.
Setting aside altogether the notorious fact that the
commercial and generally the educated classes in
Ireland are on the side of the Union—setting aside
the argument that in such questions as the framing
of a new constitution for a whole people those classes
ought to have special weight, we cannot admit
such an overwhelming preponderance, even of the
ignorant, as has been assumed.   The facts and

figures connected with the Irish elections in 1885 are in glaring contradiction to this assumption. There were 78 contested constituencies. The total number of electors in these was 585,715. Of this total only 295,269 voted for the Parnellite candidates, which is a very small majority indeed on such a total. The remaining number is made up of more than 145,000 votes given for the Unionist candidates, and the enormous number of 145,361 votes not given at all—owing to the intimidation exercised on the voters. The total majority over the Unionists, and over those who did not dare to vote, has been stated on good authority at the quite trifling amount of 4,823.[1] Nothing but the most reckless passion and fanaticism could represent such a vote as this—given under such conditions—and amongst such a population, as one which we must instantly accept as expressing the deliberate decision of the whole Irish people, and as compelling us to break up our Parliament and to rebuild our Constitution.

This wilful and passionate determination not to look even for a moment behind the polls in the Irish elections, when it is notorious that undue

[1] Irish Election Returns, 1885, L.L.P.U. Offices, Dublin.

influences were powerfully exerted there, stands out in marked contrast with the equally passionate determination to analyse in the most hostile spirit the electoral returns from Great Britain, which were at least immeasurably more honest and more independent. And this is all the more significant for us when we note the purpose or intention with which these contrasted modes of dealing stand in very clear connection. The return of some forty-five Parnellite members more than had been returned before is the ostensible ground, and the only one, upon which our invertebrate leaders defend their great change in the recognition both of duties and of facts. We do not deny that the existence of such a large party in the House of Commons which is bent on breaking up our Imperial Parliament, is a serious and a dangerous evil. But we do deny that it throws any new light whatever on the ultimate aims of that party, or on the methods which it employs. On the contrary, all the circumstances connected with its operations confirm our former estimates of that character and of those methods. Superior force or insuperable difficulties may compel us to change a policy, but it cannot justify us in following men who, without one particle of evidence, retract all that they and we have been saying for years on matters of fact and on principles of moral obligation. It is quite intolerable alike to our perceptions of truth and to our sense of duty, that on the mere fact of some forty-five men being returned by a very ignorant population, under the most violent pressure and the most immoral guidance, we should not only cease to fight, as we have long done, against the breaking up of Parliament, but that we should pretend to absolute conversion, and become the close associates and intimate allies of those whom we have so justly and so constantly denounced.

Nor is this feeling founded only on that revolt, which is right and natural, against the humiliation of conscious insincerity in ourselves and against the exhibition of irrational inconsistency in others. It is founded also on mental instincts which are inseparable from all true political faculty. In drawing up new political constitutions everything depends on our discernment of the forces operating in the Society with which we deal. Forms of government, and contrivances for the control of men, which may be quite adequate to their purpose if applied to communities in which the fundamental doctrines of civilisation have never been called in question, will be as the green withes on the limbs of Samson if these political contrivances are applied to communities honeycombed by the doctrines of anarchy.   When we resist, therefore, and protest against changes of language and of opinion so violent, so sudden, and so purely external in their causes and occasion, as the changes of our old friends in the Irish question, we are not merely revolting against these changes because they are changes, but because they betray a dangerous instability of mind on the cardinal conditions of the problem to be solved.   If the conditions of Irish Society were like the conditions of our own early colonies and plantations, in which the people accepted simply and instinctively all the traditions of personal freedom, and of respect for property and for law in which they had been born, then, indeed, we might try with a light heart even the dangerous work of dividing what had been united, and of devising new ties to keep together in some degree parts which we deliberately dissever.   But at least up to a recent moment we were consentient in declaring that we knew this not to be the case in Ireland.   The allegations of a complete and favourable change in this respect are allegations founded on no evidence whatever. On the contrary, we see that in despite of special legislation to make life artificially easier to the Irish people than to all other men, the agitators have become more and more violent, and have exhibited more and more clearly the determination ' to march through plunder to disintegration.'

We note another circumstance fatal to our confidence in the soberness of mind and judgment which can alone fit men for such a task as that which they have undertaken. Not only do they grievously misinterpret the symptoms of the present time, but their language is marked by the most passionate misrepresentations of the past. Mr. Gladstone speaks with contumely of our knowledge of history, and of our reluctance to enter upon that field with him. Not only do we repel this accusation, but, with the fullest conviction, we assert that his speeches have teemed with the most erroneous conceptions and representations on matters of historical fact. We deny altogether the justice of the picture he has drawn of the methods by which the Union was effected. On the most lenient view, it is one-sided to the most deplorable degree.

Even if it were nearer the truth than it is, it could not and ought not to affect our course. He himself professes to admit that the Union ought not to be repealed. Such great transactions as the Irish Union cannot be treated or dealt with upon the opinion we may form on the mere personal incidents or agencies which marked the conduct of them. Roman Catholics reproach the Anglican Reformation with circumstances of violence and corruption which cannot be disputed, and which we can never look back upon without condemnation and remorse. But no sudden awakening on our part to the brutalities of Henry VIII. could afford any reason at all for recalling the Reformation. The great revolution of 1688 was effected under such circumstances of personal conduct on the part of many men and of many parties that the calm and judicial spirit of Mr. Lecky has condemned it thus—'It was effected by a foreign prince with a foreign army. It was rendered possible, or at least bloodless, by an amount of aggravated treachery, duplicity, and ingratitude seldom surpassed in history.'[1] This has all the ring of Mr. Gladstone's attack upon the Union; yet no man

[1] Lecky's *History of England*, vol. i. p. 16.

in his senses would propose that on such grounds as these we should undo anything that was then done.

We hold, therefore, that the violent and most exaggerated language in which Mr. Gladstone continually speaks of the conduct of the Irish Union, is as irrelevant as it is one-sided and unjust. It is impossible to read the Cornwallis correspondence without seeing that the aims of Mr. Pitt and of his agents were at least high and noble aims ; that the influences and motives amongst Irishmen which were opposed to the Union were infinitely more corrupt than those which were in its favour; and that in so far as the means Mr. Pitt and Lord Cornwallis did employ deserved the name of corruption at all, they were used to buy up, and to buy off, the vested interests of corruption, and to close accounts with it for ever. The evidence of men as pure-minded as any amongst us now, is conclusive against the truth and justice of Mr. Gladstone's passionate declamation against the greatest of his prede-cessors. One such evidence comes from a man with whom Mr. Gladstone must have many sym-pathies—a man of such singularly independent mind that his influence on thought in England has been universally acknowledged—the once well-known Mr. Alexander Knox. No man had better opportunities of observing Irish society, and the following passage in a letter from him, dated February 14, 1800, shows the general result of his observations on the comparative morality of the two Irish parties—'I am sure Government will proceed, let the defections be ever so numerous; for a majority they will still have, in spite of both corruption and cowardice; and let that majority be ever so small, having truth and reason with them, so many of the most sensible and disinterested men in Ireland on their side, and the strength of the British Empire at their back, they would deserve to be hung up as monuments of folly and weakness if they were deterred from their purpose by the clamour of narrow-minded, interested lawyers, or the rude roar of a frantic populace. I have the pleasure of thinking that neither Lord Cornwallis nor Lord Castlereagh are very subject either to trepidation or versatility; and their friend Mr. Pitt will be as little disposed as either of them to give up Ireland to the government of selfishness and prejudice.'[1]

[1] *Remains of Alexander Knox*, vol. iv. p. 61.

It would be unreasonable to deny that a separate Parliament, which in one form or another had existed so long in Ireland, must have gathered round itself some most natural and most legitimate prepossessions.   But the evidence of a most upright man, with a wide experience, and a keen and close observation of human character, is given to us in the following words of Lord Cornwallis to Mr. Pitt: — 'That every man in this most corrupt country should consider the important question before us in no other point of view than as it may be likely to promote his own private objects of ambition or avarice will not surprise you.'[1]   This, no doubt, is the unrestrained language of private and confidential correspondence, and may probably require some qualifying words to represent facts as a whole; but there is abundant evidence that substantially it was true.

At all events, we can see that Mr. Pitt's object and his measure was directed to raise Ireland to a full share in the glories of a common empire; whilst, on the contrary, Mr. Gladstone's scheme was to degrade Ireland into a subject and a tributary province.

[1] *Cornwallis Correspondence*, vol. iii. p. 8.

Then, again, when our former leader goes further back into history, his language has been often even more glaringly and indisputably at variance with historical facts. His speech at a luncheon of Nonconformists in London, early in June 1887, was a signal proof of an excitement which seems to leave no room for the due appreciation of the facts of Irish history. That Ireland was a peaceful or happy country in any of its relations before the English invasion, and that the many troubles and difficulties of Ireland have arisen from that invasion, is in the teeth of all historical evidence. The direct contrary is the fact. Ireland was a scene of hideous barbarism before the English invasion. The best and most prosperous parts of Ireland always have been, and now are, those parts of it which have had the largest share of the invading blood, and the closest participation in its institutions and its laws.[1]   But, indeed, the whole assumptions on which alone such an assertion could be made are essentially unhistoric. There is no continuous or surviving separation between the invading and the invaded races.

---

[1] I republish in the Appendix a letter on this subject which I addressed to the *Times* on June 3, 1884.

The Celtic, Saxon, Anglo-Norman, Welsh, and Scottish bloods are all inextricably mixed and blended in the present population of Ireland ; and the attempt to revive now the animosities of vanished centuries, as a weapon of party warfare, is an attempt with which we can have no fellowship.

Then there is another ground of argument on which our judgment condemns altogether the analogies asserted between the new British Constitution invented by Mr. Gladstone to meet the case of Ireland, and any existing constitution in the world. Our own relations with our colonies have become a relation of sentiment alone, and much as we may cherish it, yet if it were to be changed, in any instance, there is not a man probably in the United Kingdom who would dream of maintaining that connection by force, or who would regard a formal separation as involving any danger to our national life. Our relations with our large self-governing colonies are, after all, as they now stand, a thing of yesterday. There are not wanting symptoms of danger even now, wherever any obvious motive of self-interest comes into play. The adoption by some of them of fiscal systems which are certainly more or less injurious to the mother country, is already regarded with strong disapprobation by large parties here, and men are beginning to ask whether the responsibilities of defence, which in certain cases might be most onerous, are to lie heavily upon us whilst our people are shut out from the markets of those for whom they may be called to fight. Even, therefore, if the Gladstonian constitution devised for Ireland had been really analogous to that which governs our relations with Canada or Australia, the application of it to one of the three kingdoms would have involved wholly different kinds and degrees of danger and of risk. But after all there is no such analogy between the two systems of political adjustment. Not one of our colonies would listen for a moment to the Gladstonian constitution as applicable to themselves.

Nor can much encouragement be derived from the only case in which we have attempted to draw up a Federal Constitution for the juvenile communities which have sprung from us. The Dominion of Canada is still only just cutting its teeth, and even already there are symptoms that on the slightest temptations those teeth will be, or may be, used in severing the ties which have been laboriously devised to bind the Provinces together. In a recent conference of the Provincial Prime Ministers a pronounced tendency has been shown to protest against the very moderate amount of power which has been assigned to the central or Dominion Ministry. That any British statesman should even talk of these new and faltering experiments in North America as affording any lesson or example to us in the United Kingdom, is a signal illustration of the depth to which our Separatists have fallen in the elements of political knowledge.

When we turn to foreign countries such analogies as really exist are wholly condemnatory of such a scheme. The Austro-Hungarian Constitution is also a thing of yesterday, and no man can tell how it will work when certain kinds of strain are brought to bear upon it. It is impossible to read the interesting volume lately published by Mr. de Lavelaye on the condition of south-eastern Europe, without seeing that the fanaticism of separate petty nationalities is introducing elements capable of the most dangerous development. But in that case there is one element of strength with which we have nothing to compare. The Hungarian portions of the Austrian Empire are still to a large extent in a very primitive condition. The loyal attachment of these people to the line and lineage of their ancient Kings is perhaps less strong than when the famous 'Moriamur' was shouted in the ears of Maria Theresa. But it is still a tie of enormous value. Is there anything to represent it among the Irish people?

But the great Continental case which really does teach an important lesson is the case of Italy. I have seen with astonishment lately that one of the group of men who have been building a shanty-constitution for us to replace the spacious palaces of our ancient laws, has quoted the case of Italy as a case proving the value of nationality. This is thoroughly in the spirit of the leader who describes the laws of Britain as laws 'foreign' to the people of Ireland. The whole force of any illustration drawn from Italian nationality depends on the idea that we stand in the same relation to Ireland that the hated 'Tedeschi' stood to Italy. Can any misrepresentation of facts be more glaring? Setting aside, on the one hand, the well-marked and sharply-defined separation of race and language between the German and the Italian people ; setting aside, on the other hand, the complete amalgamation of races which exists between us and Ireland, we must ask was Italy ever represented freely and fully in a German or Imperial Parliament ? Was that a case of 'Union,' however halting or imperfect ? And is it not an insult, then, to our understandings to compare the relations between Germany and Italy with the relations between Great Britain and Ireland as having the slightest bearing on each other ?

But there is another aspect in which the case of Italy does bear, and bears most impressively, on the Irish question, because it bears on the nobler senses in which nationality may be understood, and the nobler purposes to which a really national sentiment may be turned. Until our own days Italy was, what Prince Metternich called it, a 'geographical expression.' It was an agglomeration of small distinct states with separate governments. Many of these had a very ancient, and in some respects a very noble history. They had produced great men, and had each taken some distinctive part in the revived glories of Literature and of Art. They had taken captive their fierce conquerors by the spells of beauty and of genius. Italy is full of towns and cities which, ever since the decline and fall of the Roman Empire, have had a more or less separate existence, sometimes as republics, sometimes as principalities, with a separate and seldom an inglorious history. Down to the present day they have cherished the memory of all who 'at sundry times and in divers manners' have rendered their names illustrious, even of those who, despite some special favours, may have been the oppressors of their race. It is thus that Pisa keeps in her Campo Santo, amidst the tombs of her own most fair Italian names, the simple but impressive image of the sleeping Barbarossa. Yet these are the very towns, and cities, and states, which have sacrificed all their separate and proud traditions, and have laid them down as a splendid sacrifice of true patriotism at the feet of one United Kingdom.

Mr. Gladstone himself, as an individual rather than as a statesman—but perhaps not on that account less effectively—has taken an honourable and unforgotten part in the accomplishment of Italian Unity. On this account alone every Italian knows and loves his name. No one can know better than he what would be the attitude of Italian statesmen

if he were to incite the now united provinces and
states of that country to set up separate parliaments and separate executive governments in Milan,
in Turin, in Venice, in Florence, and in Palermo.
And yet few men think or consider enough, how
much—how very much—many of these famous
places have sacrificed to the cause of Italian Unity.
Their grass-grown streets, their mouldering palaces,
their empty theatres, their silent halls once filled
with the proud councillors of splendid municipali-
ties, testify to the sad changes which are sometimes
inseparable from the progress or consolidation of
great nations.

No such sacrifice has Ireland, or any part of it,
been ever called to make.   In Ireland there have
been no ancient, free, and famous towns—no great
centres of civilisation or of achievement—either in
arts or arms—since the glow-worm lamps of her early
Celtic Church were merged, more than a thousand
years ago, in the common altar flame of Latin Christianity.   Let us hear what an enthusiastic Irishman
confesses respecting the nationality of Ireland, when
his eyes are opened to see, and his mouth is opened
to speak, the truth, by the desire to condemn a
passionate and injurious phrase long since happily

forgotten : ' Now the " Irish Enemy " was no nation in the modern sense of the word, but a race divided into many nations or tribes, separately defending their lands from English Barons in their immediate neighbourhood. There had been no ancient national government displaced, no national dynasty overthrown ; the Irish had no national flag, nor any capital city as the metropolis of their common country, nor any common administration of law ; nor did they ever give a combined opposition to the English. The English coming in the name of the Pope, with the aid of the Irish Bishops, and with a superior national organisation, which the Irish easily recognised, were accepted by the Irish. Neither King Henry II. nor King John ever fought a battle in Ireland.' [1]

All this, and a great deal more than this, is true, and establishes the great modifications of meaning in which alone we can apply the word ' nation ' to Ireland as a whole. So far as race and predominant language are concerned, there has been a complete amalgamation. The descendants of the conquerors and the conquered have been inextricably mixed. If the Italian states and provinces, with

[1] Prendergast's *Cromwellian Settlement*, p. 28.

their illustrious, and in some cases their glorious, history, have been proud to give up all their separate Governments in order to make one powerful nation, we ask absolutely nothing in the way of sacrifice when we ask the Irish to forget the anarchy of their clans—their fierce and ceaseless intertribal wars— their long centuries of mutual devastation and bloodshed—and to join with pride and thankfulness in the work of Government under a Constitution which respects all the just rights, and all the true liberties of men. In denying to them, on the ground of historical fact and of political development, the character of a separate Nationality, we are not at all denying any of those peculiarities of mind, or of disposition, or of character, which may often become well marked and distinct in societies of men who are separated from others by nothing but a river, or a hill, or a narrow channel of the sea. We recognise in this sense, and in this degree, some well-marked characteristics distinguishing, not so much Ireland as a whole, as different parts of Ireland, and we desire to retain these characteristics as valuable elements in the service of our common Empire. We point to the indisputable fact that among the Irishmen who have been illustrious in

any of the walks of life, there has been a happy and
indiscriminate mingling of Celtic and of Saxon
names.   So far as any distinctions of mere race or
of origin are concerned, there is not a shadow of
excuse for the breaking-up of our United Parliament.

But whilst the splendid case of Italian unity,
which our separatist politicians have so audaciously
referred to, is a case which tells so conclusively
against them, there is another case in some respects
more cognate, which is not less valuable in point-
ing our moral against the disruptive policy.   It is
the case of the United States.   Immense and
innumerable as are the differences between the
long historical development of the United Kingdom, and the sudden clustering of separate colonies,
which were fused and welded into one great nation
under the heat and pressure of a common war for
a common independence, there is one difference
which is above and before all others.   The Colonies
were communities of men who had not then even
begun to question the fundamental doctrines of
civilisation.   They were in full possession and in
the full enjoyment of all the traditions of English
liberty—of English independence.   They respected

individual freedom ; they respected property ; they upheld good faith in the deliberate agreements between man and man ; they protected life from violence, whether of the few or of the many ; they maintained, above all things, as the foundation of all liberty, the sanctity and authority of law.

Therefore it was that in first framing a common federation among themselves, it did not even occur to them, at the moment, that special provisions could be required to provide against any departure from the primary obligations of all civilised societies. But when this duty was forced upon them by the necessity of framing a more complete and systematic constitution, then, indeed, they set themselves to the work with a dignity, sobriety, and wisdom, which are all in striking contrast with the hurry, passion, shallowness, and levity that have marked the birth of our new British Constitution, and the language and conduct of its master-builders. These men knew, and had repeatedly declared, that the Irish Parnellite party did not hold to the accepted duties and obligations of civilised society ; yet they did not provide in the new Constitution any adequate securities for life, liberty, or property. As regards the most salient points of all political organisations—such as whether it was to be federal or not, whether there was to be a full or a partial representation of Ireland in Imperial councils, or none at all— these wonderful architects proposed one thing one day, and intimated that they withdrew it the next. Even now they are stumping the country with a cynical refusal to tell us what they mean. The obvious truth is that they have not the remotest idea themselves of anything, except trust in a few empty phrases, and a servile confidence in one man. The wonderful mastery of the subject which they have already shown is pleaded as the ground of an implicit and perfect confidence in themselves. Our demand that before we pull down the old palaces of our Constitution we should know at least the main lines of the new buildings which are to hold us in their stead, is, treated as a trap into which they will not walk. Or if, by extreme condescension on their part, they tell us what their principle is, that principle is expressed in some one or more of those vague phrases which Mr. Gladstone himself denounced not long ago as phrases which may mean anything or nothing.

All this represents a condition of things which

seems almost incredible. It is not—with us who see the position of affairs in this light—a question of mere expedience or policy, whether we should support the Separatists or not. It is a question involving moral obligations of the most binding character. We cannot follow where duties confessed yesterday are repudiated to-day. We cannot assent to proposals involving the fate of our fellow-subjects in all the dearest interests of their life, and which are yet studiously concealed in a cloud of words not susceptible of any definite interpretation.

And if anything could be added to intensify our revolt against the sacrifice of duty which is thus demanded of us—if anything could deepen our distrust of those who make it, this aggravation would be found in their gratuitous attempt to rouse up Scotland, and also Wales, to ask for separation as if it were a boon—as something of advantage which, if Ireland gets it, they also ought to ask. Our former leader, in the days when he was opposing Home Rule, used the argument which had often been used before, and has often been used since—the argument summed up in Canning's famous exclamation, 'Repeal the Union!

Restore the Heptarchy!' Mr. Gladstone used it, or appeared to use it, as regards Scotland and Wales, precisely as others had used it as a *reductio ad absurdum*. But that argument, as used by him, is now interpreted as having been intended to lay it down as a principle that, under like conditions of popular demand, the same provisions for Home Rule which may be applicable to Ireland might be equally applicable to all the four 'well-marked nationalities' into which, in imagination, he disintegrates the United Kingdom.

As a Scotchman whose ancestors did something towards bringing about the Union, and who, with the great body of the Scottish people, has been accustomed to rejoice in, and to be proud of, its results, I cannot express in the ordinary language of political discussion the feelings with which we have regarded the very idea of a change which would remove our members from the Imperial Legislature, either altogether or at all times except when called in to vote upon customs and excise. We have not so learned our privileges and our duty. We are an integral party of the Empire—loyal to it, proud of it, and determined not to be bribed, by any mean desire, to sacrifice our full share in its glories or its responsibilities. We regard the very thought of such a surrender as due to some form of madness. It is indeed just possible that even a wise and dispassionate mind might conceive or evolve such a project as this if the experiment had been well elaborated, and if it had been tried and crowned with unquestionable success in Ireland. But we regard with feelings little short of reprobation the fact that any responsible statesman should talk in this loose way of the most profound organic changes affecting the three kingdoms, when his own plan for one of them had hopelessly broken down, both in Parliament and at the polls of a General Election—when it had broken down not merely in the sense of having been defeated, but in the sense of having been abandoned and disclaimed by its own authors, who shouted loudly to all concerned that they did not and could not ask it to be sanctioned.

Such methods of proceeding are alien to the whole nature and history of our political Institutions. Nor is it made better by the spirit which is, we think, distinctly perceptible in the language employed. That language has had a taint of menace and of vindictiveness in it which closely resembles the spirit in which Irish landowners were warned and threatened for not accepting the partial or total expropriation which was offered as a boon. In like manner we have been warned that if we do not allow the separate Parliament for Ireland, a larger and wider demand will be made upon us, and that when men's minds are roused by prolonged controversy upon proposals which ought to have been accepted meekly, we shall find them pressed further and further, to our discomfiture and dismay.

We protest against this method of political controversy anywhere, but especially in an old Constitutional country, where free debate has been wont to be held, and where high questions of human Government have hitherto been dealt with safe from revolutionary menace. At all events we declare that we are not to be intimidated by threats. We must do our duty in contending against proposals which we think most injurious, and we shall rely on the intelligence of our fellow-subjects to withhold their confidence from men who adopt such methods of political action.

And, further, as we protest against menace, so also do we protest against cajolery, merging into a

new and most insidious form of political corruption.
It is absolutely new in our honoured history that
party leaders should put up to the auction of votes
on some one political question, the fate of other laws
and other institutions on which, at the same time,
they decline to commit themselves to any definite
policy.   The grosser forms of bribery, of which
Mr. Pitt is accused in carrying the Union (even if
the accusation were true, which it is not) are innocence itself compared with the demoralisation
involved in hiring men to vote for the breaking
up of our United Parliament by holding out to
them vague hopes and expectations that if they do
so they will, or at least may, get disestablisment of
the Church, or some other equally irrelevant object
of political agitation or desire.   Yet this is the
kind of bribery which has been systematically pursued.   Every fraction of a party, anywhere, which
has some object to gain, some theory to push, some
advantage to secure, is stimulated and encouraged
to keep its own fad in view, and in the running,
by the one grand panacea for all ills, namely,
by bringing back the Anglo-Parnellites into office.
Again I say, that without judging the morals of
other men, or how far excuses, which we think

delusions, may hide from them the real character of such tactics, we declare emphatically that to us, and for us, any fellowship with it would be dishonest.

But the moral, or rather the immoral, elements which revolt us in the conduct of the new scheme for breaking up the Imperial Parliament, might not of themselves be conclusive arguments against it. Such elements have appeared, and may appear again, in connection with great changes which have been on the whole reforms. We dwell, therefore, with more emphasis on those other elements of objection resting purely upon evidence and upon reasoning,—which appear to us to be of overwhelming force. The first demand we make, not only upon others but on ourselves, is that the facts with which we have to deal should be acknowledged and looked at in the face. Before giving up to the rule of a separate Parliament and a separate Executive the whole people of one of our three United Kingdoms, we insist that the conditions of Society as now existing there should be taken into account. These conditions represent the forces to which the new Constitution must be adapted, so that they may be yoked to service in the interests of righteousness and of justice—of truth and honesty, and of that personal liberty without which life would be intolerable.

Most fortunately we find that respecting those conditions of Society the evidence is abundant and conclusive. Moreover, we find the best summary of that evidence in the witness borne by the very men who are now our chief opponents. We don't care the least to convict them of any mere personal inconsistency in matters of opinion, or of sentiment. We might as well reproach chameleons with inconsistency, because of changes in the colour of their skins, as reproach our former friends and colleagues of the Parnellite Alliance because of the metamorphoses through which they have lately passed. But we are determined to weigh, and to examine with the closest attention, those facts of Irish Society on which the testimony of these very men has been the most recent and the most authentic.

In a previous page I have spoken of that testimony as we have it in the conduct and language of the Irish Secretary during the three years between the passing of the Prevention of Crimes Act in 1882 and the fall of the Gladstone Administration in June 1885. There is no evidence so responsible

and authentic as that of men charged with the
actual administration of such a law, having such
an object, and called upon, night after night, to
answer in the face of our Parliament, which is in
the face of the world, the questioning of the Irish
Nationalist party. Platform speeches may be good
for nothing, or good for very little. But here we
have from a responsible minister and an honourable man, the doings, the sayings, the admissions,
the declarations on matters of fact, which present
us with a vivid picture of the condition of
Ireland, and of the temper and spirit of those
whose chief business it was to thwart the Government in working any Act for the prevention of
crime. Let us take out of this wide and dreadful
canvas, almost at random, some portions of the
scene which is depicted on it. Let one be a sketch
of the condition of a considerable district and community; let another be an illustration of the daily
life of individual men as it is led under the tyranny
of village tyrants ; and let the last bring home to
us the animus and language of those to whose rule,
constituted into a separate Parliament, we are
asked to deliver Ireland.

On the 19th of April 1883 Mr. Trevelyan,

fiercely questioned in the House of Commons by an Irish member, had to tell the House that in the district of Loughrea, in Galway, no less than eight deliberate murders had been committed within the period of one year ; that a movement had lately been started there—by persons strongly suspected of being members of a secret society for purposes of murder, and who had actually been in prison on that suspicion—with the object of collecting funds for the baffling of justice, but nominally for the defence of all who might be arrested and charged with crime ; that these persons had resolved to make a house-to-house visitation over the country ; that the terror exercised by them was such that the farmers dared not refuse, although unwilling to give them money ; that the mere fact of such men demanding money was of itself intimidation when made to defenceless farmers ; that the unfortunate peasants had appealed to the Government for protection ; and that the measures taken by the Executive were the very minimum of what were required for preserving the peace of the district.[1]

Just let us conceive, if we can, the condition of honest men living in such a district as this,—com-

[1] *Hansard*, vol. 278, pp. 617-18.

pelled to subsidise their tyrants: their relations, or their servants, or their friends, murdered in numbers, and in cold blood, in the fields and lanes and cottages around them, the perpetrators probably perfectly well known, but unpunished, and enjoying not only absolute impunity, but the exercise of supreme power through the terror they inspired. Just let us think what all this implies— of the wickedness of some, of the tame submission of others, of the complete disorganisation of Society, of the fitness of such a community for the exercise of the highest administrative authority, and of the animus of those members of the House of Commons who attacked the Government for protecting the people from a most cruel and a most criminal organisation.

And now, passing from the description of wide districts such as this in Galway, let us look at the details of individual life—if life it can be called, when it is passed under the cruel tyrannies of the Nationalist party. Four months later, in the same session, on the 23d of August 1883, Mr. Trevelyan was, in pursuance of an almost daily practice, savagely attacked for the endeavours of the Irish Government to secure the ' Prevention of Crime.'

On this occasion he had a most typical and a most pathetic tale to tell. At a place with the characteristic name of Aughabullogue there lived a tradesman, a blacksmith, of the name of Hallissey. He was an honest and industrious man, earning about 35s. a week in the exercise of his calling. That calling of necessity brought him into relations of custom with all classes and conditions of society around him. All of these he served faithfully and honestly without distinction, as it was his duty to do. But that which was his duty to the community was a crime against the League. He shod the horses, he mended the ploughs, of all who came to him, and amongst others, of those who were persecuted by the local tyrants. He was warned not to do his duty, but he had the virtue and the courage to continue doing it. For this crime he was, by the processes of boycotting, reduced to penury. Two neighbours, kinder than the rest, had done him some little service, and for this offence their implements were broken and destroyed. Even the doctor was afraid to visit him when he was ill. Still holding out, he became the victim of still more active measures. Standing at his own door he was struck senseless by a stone. Actively or passively, the whole population round him were implicated in one great conspiracy to ruin one good and brave man. The case was brought to the knowledge of the Irish Government. 'It became necessary,' said Mr. Trevelyan in the House of Commons, 'to show that, as in England and in Scotland, a citizen who did his duty by the community had a right to live.'[1] A body of police was stationed in, and charged upon, the district, for the protection of this man's life, and as an expression of the opinion of the Queen's Government on his loyalty to law and order, and on its own duty in upholding him. At last the parish priest, powerless apparently to do anything better, opened a subscription to get this brave man removed from the parish altogether. The local authorities, after some twelve months had elapsed, and no improvement had been effected, were willing to accept this solution of the difficulty. Nothing but exile from his home, nothing but the removal from out of their very sight of such a man, could appease or satisfy the vindictive hatred of the League.

But the most memorable fact is that the feeling

[1] *Hansard*, vol. 283, p. 1783.

of this conspiracy was fully shared and openly expressed by the Irish party in the House of Commons. Everything that the Government had done for the protection of this brave man was an offence to them. One of them called poor Hallissey a 'ruffian,' and another said that something might be said for the migration scheme if it was used for the purpose of ridding the country of citizens like Hallissey. Mr. Trevelyan was roused by this. His language was temperate, and carefully restrained. But it was significant. He exclaimed, ' What a really terrible sentiment that was ! What was Hallissey's fault? Why, that he had done his duty as an honest tradesman, and as a fearless citizen.' [1]

Here then we have two cases, out of hundreds more, affording most convincing and far-reaching evidence on the condition not only of Galway— not only of ' Aughabullogue ' — but of a great part of Ireland. The Nationalist members in the Parliament of 1885 evinced by every sign of speech and gesture, by shouts and interruptions, complete sympathy with the agencies which coerced the farmers of Loughrea and persecuted the brave

[1] *Hansard*, vol. 283, p. 1784.

blacksmith of Aughabullogue. These members have since been reinforced by some forty or more additional members with the same sympathies and the same antipathies. Can it be affirmed with any confidence that the return of these men has been independent of the same agencies of intimidation under which we thus see that whole districts tremble, and brave men who dare to resist can only be saved by exile? Is it not worse than a farce to talk to us of the 'rooted desires' of the Irish people being represented by elections conducted under such conditions of society? Is it possible for us who have been brought up in the traditions of British liberty and law to change by one hair's-breadth our opinion on the duty of upholding those traditions because some forty more men have been elected, under such influences, to claim through a separate government the power of enforcing upon our fellow-subjects in Ireland those sentiments which Mr. Trevelyan was constrained, most justly, to denounce as ' terrible '?

But we turn from mere local evidence to the evidence supplied of the same spirit in the House of Commons, as testified by the Irish Secretary.

On another occasion — in August 1883 — that Minister declared that, after watching for fifteen months the condition of mind evinced by the Irish party, he could only conclude that they objected to everything done for the prevention of crime. Their remarks, he said, had been one long palliation of every one who had been convicted of crime, with accusations couched in very severe and unjust terms against every one who had been concerned in bringing criminals to justice, from the judge to the jurymen in the box, and against all the counsel and witnesses who had been concerned.

On another occasion, in October 1884, Mr. Gladstone himself was obliged to intervene in defence of Lord Spencer, and in rebuke of the Irish Members who reprobated his action in the case of the atrocious murders in the 'Joyce Country.' So utterly alien were the tone and words of the Irish Members to all that in Great Britain we have been accustomed to revere, that the Prime Minister told them that in such words 'they speak to us in a foreign language.' [1]

Perhaps even more significant, as bearing upon

[1] *Hansard*, vol. 293, p. 365.

the character of the Nationalist party in Parliament, and upon the impression it produced upon honourable men who were brought into contact with them, was another passage in one of the replies of Mr. Trevelyan. This was in the same month, August 1883. He spoke of the odiousness of the duty thrown upon him day after day in having to repel attacks upon every effort of the Government to repress or to punish crime. But he expressed at the same time almost a sense of pride and gratitude that the honour of such a work had fallen to his lot. Yes! But the measure of this honour was the measure of the immorality of those against whom it had to be endured.

We agree with Mr. Trevelyan that it was a duty and that it was an honour. But we disagree with him in holding that it has ceased to be a duty and an honour now. That the Ministers who held this language up to Midsummer 1885 should now be in close alliance with the men of whom they spoke in such terms, is a fact fortunately without parallel in our political history.

But this is not the consideration which dwells most upon our minds. We are not swayed by any opinion on the conduct of individual men.

They are, or may be, the mere bubbles on the surface of a deeper stream. We look simply at the matter as one of evidence—as proving what we have the best reason to expect from a separate Parliament and a separate Executive in Ireland. We see that the political forces with which we have to contend in Ireland are immoral and anarchic. We see that the Nationalist party do not accept the fundamental doctrines of civilised societies. We see that they support and defend, or excuse, the most cruel tyranny —that they denounce as 'ruffians' men who are brave, and honest, and faithful in the discharge of duty to all their neighbours, without distinction of party. We see that institutions, and processes of administration, and forms of Government which may not only be plausible upon paper, but which might work fairly well for a people which is virtuous and law-abiding, and loyal to the authority of an Imperial Jurisprudence, will be utterly unsuited to bear the stress and strain of such conditions of society as those which are thus proved to exist in Ireland. Presumptuous as— under any circumstances—we should have deemed the conduct of men who set themselves in a few weeks to go 'down to the very roots' of an ancient Constitution—to grub them up, and to lay them down again cut, and shaped, and pruned at their will and pleasure—we condemn this presumption still more severely when we consider the nature of the problem which they well knew they had to solve.

But this is not all that we have to say—because it is not the only, nor the last, nor the worst offence which we have to charge against our former associates. If they had a plan by which they themselves are willing to abide—however weak we might deem that plan to be—we might understand and excuse any amount of confidence in it, and any amount of persistence in their recommendation of it. But their present position is to patronise and adopt the whole tone and temper of the Nationalist party in resisting and denouncing the very measures for the Prevention of Crime, and for the protection of innocence, that they were themselves executing and defending in the loftiest language a few months ago, whilst at the same time no two of them are agreed upon the most essential features of any new Constitution for re-soldering a broken Parliament and a disunited kingdom. They are united in nothing but in a series of empty phrases, the whole value of which lies in their boundless latitude of meaning—phrases identical with those which their Leader used to denounce for years, for this very reason, that in some senses they might be 'perfectably acceptable and even desirable,' whilst in others they would be 'mischievous and revolutionary.' It seems to be a direct policy and device for the concealment of this dissentience, and ignorance, and irresolution amongst themselves, that they are now uniting in attacks upon the Government for doing exactly what they acknowledged to be their own duty when they were in office.

There are in this world some sayings that cannot be unsaid. They were either true or untrue. If they were ever true, they remain true for all time, because they are moral truths—truths affecting duty and insuperable moral obligations. Most legitimate, indeed, is that operation of the mind by which we may be led to drop the use of arguments of policy with which we have ourselves ceased to be wholly satisfied. But most illegitimate, on the other hand, is that other operation by which we are tempted to hide, or to gloss over, facts and obligations which have ceased to be convenient for some present purpose. Both moral

and intellectual integrity are thus sacrificed to
tactics. Those assertions of fact which were put
into the mouth of the Sovereign upon a most
momentous issue in January 1881, and the personal
repetitions of them which in later consecutive years
were continued with reiteration and with passion,
were assertions of indisputable truth. It was truth,
moreover, not only relevant, but fundamental in
the subject matter. It concerned the temper, the
purposes, the designs, with which a separate Parliament is sought for Ireland. It concerned, therefore, the essential conditions, and the special difficulties besetting any attempt to limit that demand, or
to control the working of the new machinery which
concession necessarily involves. It was truth in
short that concerned the very possibility of defending
effectually the social interests which must be placed
in direst jeopardy. We were consentient with our
former leader in the emphasis he laid on this truth.
We were consentient with him also, when he added
to many other most just indictments the significant
observation that the Irish leader, in all his very
copious references to America as the only friend of
Ireland, ' had never found time to utter one word
of disapproval of, or misgiving about, what is

known as the assassination literature of that country.'[1] This observation has been the germ of the later and copious literature on the connection between ' Parnellism and Crime.' It involved and rested on the sound principle that political leaders are largely responsible for the action and the language of their followers. It laid down the doctrine, too—not less important—that they may be deeply responsible not only for speech, but for silence. We were consentient with him in this important teaching, and we are consentient still.

Nor does our consentience with our old leader end with this. There was a striking passage, quite prophetic, in one of his Midlothian speeches during the General Election in November 1885. It was delivered in the Albert Hall on the 9th of that month. He was referring to the possibility of the Liberal party being called upon to deal with this great constitutional question of the government of Ireland in a position where it was only a minority dependent on the Irish vote for converting it into a majority, and he proceeded thus: — ' Now, gentlemen, I tell you

[1] *Times*, October 8, 1881. Speech at Leeds.

seriously and solemnly that although I believe the Liberal party itself to be honourable, patriotic, sound, and trustworthy, yet in such a position it would not be trustworthy. In such a position as that it would not be safe to enter upon the consideration of the principles of a measure with respect to which at every step of its progress it would be in the power of a party coming from Ireland to say "unless you do this, and unless you do that, we turn you out to-morrow."[1]

This is exactly what has happened. The prophet has had the power to fulfil his own prediction. A few leaders of the Liberal party have fallen with him under this foreseen temptation. They have not been trustworthy. They have carried with them — reluctant, helpless, struggling, distracted, protesting, and openly dissentient on points of primary importance — a large number of old adherents. The former leader has now to confess that his following is 'a shattered and disunited party.'[2] It is so, because they have been led against the impregnable batteries of truth and duty. Fortunately not a few of our former

[1] *Fourth Midlothian Campaign*, p. 29.
[2] *Lessons of the Elections*, p. 27.

leaders, and some of the very best, are our leaders still. Our former friends have left the great cause in which we fought together. From that cause they have been deserters. In so deserting we think they have been untrue to the great traditions of public virtue without which freedom and liberty are but empty names. We remain consentient with those traditions. We are consentient with all the great men, and with all the great generations, which have built up the polity of one great Empire out of three United Kingdoms. We shall respond to any, and to every appeal which may be made to us to consider this tremendous subject of Irish government in a reverent and a reasonable spirit. Nothing should be refused to Ireland which in itself is just. In Education, for example, as one great subject of local government, I think we have failed, and Mr. Gladstone has failed, conspicuously. But we recognise no such reasonable spirit in the demand of any man, or of any party, to be allowed to dig down to the ' very roots of our Constitution both civil and political,' upon a claim of purely personal confidence. Still less do we recognise any such spirit in a haughty refusal to tell us what they mean to

I

do, or to propose, when they have been hoisted into power. Our demand to know all this beforehand is a demand upon which it is our duty to insist. That it should be refused and resisted as a ' trap ' seems to us to be unjustifiable in the highest degree. If Party leaders have rights, they have also duties. It is not one of those duties to start suddenly upon the people of this country a new paper-constitution, which its author admits to involve principles as absolutely novel to them as the differential calculus. We have now had time to look at that production, round and round. We see that it involves proposals which offend our reason, and which revolt our conscience.

APPENDIX

APPENDIX.

THE NEW EDUCATION.

To the Editor of the 'Times.'

Sir,—Our friends the Parnellite Liberals, under great Parliamentary discouragement, have gallantly announced it as their mission to 'educate the country.' In the discharge of this mission their handling of facts deserves attention. I am not sure that 'the masses' care much for ancient, or even for recent, history, but they are under the sway of it none the less. Obscure memories and hereditary traditions are the real source of living and powerful social forces. The Parnellite missionaries know this well. Belonging themselves generally to 'the classes,' they do not affect to despise history. What they do is to re-write it in their own sense; and certainly nothing can be more splendid than the freedom and the dash with which they handle it. If the 'education of our masters' has become a public duty, assuredly the watching of our new professors has risen to the rank of an absolute necessity.

Mr. Gladstone's recent speech at a meeting of Nonconformists contained two historical assertions, or representations of historical fact, which seem to me to be demonstrably erroneous. The first is that the miseries of Ireland began with, or were aggravated by, the English invasion. The second is that the Irish Roman Catholics, when they had the power, have never shown a disposition to religious persecution, or have shown much less disposition to it than their Protestant opponents. I do not stop to discuss how far, or to what extent, these assertions are relevant to the great constitutional questions now before us. Be that relevancy great or small, all I say is that they are without any historical foundation, and are not merely caricatures, but complete contradictions of the truth.

In the long history of political extravagance, I doubt if any sentence of any responsible speaker could be found to match the following :—

'Who made the Irishman? The Irish in very old times indeed, if you go back to the earlier stages of Christianity, were among the leaders of Christendom. But we went in among them ; we sent among them numbers of our own race. These were mixed with the Irish, and ever since our blood has been united with theirs there has been this endless trouble and difficulty.'

The blessedness of Irish Celtic society before the taint of Anglo-Saxon blood came in to corrupt it would be an historical discovery indeed, if only it could be verified. But, unfortunately for this theory, it is not only incapable of proof, but it is susceptible of the completest refutation. It is

true, indeed, that in a remote age, many centuries
before the English invasion, there was an early
branch of the Christian Church planted in Ireland,
the memory of whose apostles is still preserved in
the old title of the ' Isle of Saints.' It appeals most
naturally to Mr. Gladstone's imagination, and it
has engendered there a mythical development more
wonderful than any of its own legendary miracles.
Far be it from me to deny the interest which
attaches to its history ; but that interest is nothing
to the purpose. Not only had the golden age
of that old Celtic Church passed away centuries
before the English invasion, but we have abundant evidence that it never had been of a kind to
justify the suggestions of the orator. The truth is
that the high but very special civilisation of the
early Scoto-Irish Celts is one of the most singular
in the history of the world. It shines across the
ages with a pure and brilliant light. But it shines
only from and upon the altar. It spent itself wholly
in the great work of spreading Christianity among
heathen tribes. Even in this work its fame is
largely founded on the achievements of its Scottish
offshoot at Iona. This, indeed, is glory enough for
any church ; but it did not indicate in the races
among whom that Church arose, nor did it impart
to them, any aptitude for civilised political institutions. Beyond the sphere of its spiritual operations
it has left no memorials of itself, except, in a later
age, some fine work in gold and jewels, lavished
upon crosiers, upon the covering of psalters, upon

missals, upon shrines, and other insignia of Christian belief. But with all its religious devotion and all its efflorescence in a peculiar and local art, the clergy who were its priests and prophets seem to have taken little heed of the social condition or of the secular affairs of the people among whom they laboured. The old Celtic monastic institutions were tribal in their organisation, and all the customs and habits of the Irish tribes were barbarous and savage in the highest degree. The glimpses we get of them in the very earliest centuries are truly horrible. In the seventh century an Abbot of Iona interfered to prevent women from being regularly enlisted in the fighting hosts, and from stabbing and tearing each other's breasts with reaping hooks. Between that date and the English invasion there elapsed somewhere about five hundred years. Before that time the old Celtic Church had been merged in the general advance of Latin Christianity. But as regards the condition of the bulk of the people in Ireland no change could possibly be a change for the worse to them. They were equally the victims of most oppressive usages in times of peace, and of the most barbarous ferocity in times of war. The first foreign invasion came at the express invitation of one of the Irish chiefs, Dermot, "King" of Leinster, and this invitation was addressed to Welshmen—another branch of the Celtic stock. In the contests which followed, this same Dermot exhibited an almost incredible barbarity towards his own countrymen to whom he had been opposed. It is not a Protestant but a Catholic historian who gives the most graphic account of the conduct of this native Irish chief. We are told that when the men of Ossory had been borne to the ground by a charge of the English cavalry, ' the fallen were immediately despatched by their compatriot Celts under the banner of Dermot. A trophy of two hundred heads was erected at the feet of that fine example of civilisation which flourished in Ireland before the Saxon invasion. He testified his joy over this hideous heap by clapping his hands, leaping in the air, and pouring out thanksgiving to the Almighty. As he tossed it over he discovered the head of a former enemy. His hatred was rekindled at the sight, and seizing it by the ears in a paroxysm of fury, he tore off the nose with his teeth.' (Lingard.)

Among the many delusions which a false sentiment has promoted there has, perhaps, never been a delusion more complete than that which imagines that in early Celtic customs and traditions, as distinguished from the corresponding customs of the Teutonic nations, there was any element which, if it had been left alone, would have built up some polity better for the mass of the people than the polity which actually arose out of the amalgamation of the races in England and in Scotland. It is quite true that the monks and priests of the early Irish Church had some culture and some letters—in a literature, moreover, which was purely Celtic — at a time when other European nations were either sunk in ignorance, or at least were so little

advanced as to have nothing of the same kind.
But from this very fact we have an amount
of evidence in respect to the conditions and
habits of those Celts which we do not possess in
respect to any other European race at the same
date. In the *Annals of the Four Masters* we have
a continuous chronicle, which there is reasonable
ground for believing to be authentic, from the
second century. The result is to show that not
only were the whole conditions of society barbarous
in the sense of being rude, rough, and violent, but
that they were barbarous in the sense of being
exceptionally savage, and without a trace of progress
towards better things. No nobler passions are
exhibited than the mere thirst for blood and the
mere triumphs of revenge. We may turn over
page after page without seeing one solitary symptom
of the crystallising forces which alone can build up
the organic structures of civilisation. There is
nothing but a sickening repetition of intertribal
battles, murders, and devastations. For seven
hundred years before the invasion of Henry, not
one single step can be traced in the path of progress.
On the contrary, the country was getting worse and
worse. There is some poetry, some feeling for
nature, especially in its wilder aspects, but the
animating spirit is almost purely ferocious, with
nothing of the higher sentiment which we understand as patriotism. No deeds of massacre, however dreadful, are ever narrated with rebuke, still
less any acts of mere plunder—unless, perchance,

any of these acts were directed against ecclesiastics. Then, indeed, the culprit king or chief is denounced as a monster, and some rival chief is incited in furious appeals to punish him with death and the devastation of his country.

Such is the paradise which Mr. Gladstone represents as having been invaded and destroyed by the intrusion of the Anglo-Saxon. Authentic history informs us, on the contrary, that the first foundations of a civilised condition were laid within ' the Pale ;' while industry and comfort have advanced elsewhere always in exact proportion with the plantation and diffusion of the same mixed races which constitute the people of Great Britain.

The other assertion of Mr. Gladstone—that the Irish people has never shown any disposition to religious persecution against Protestants comparable with that which has been shown by Protestants against Irish Catholics—is a representation of historical fact which is as absolutely erroneous as the other. Macaulay's powerful description and denunciation of the proceedings of the Irish Parliament in 1689, when the Catholics were supreme, puts an end to this pretension. In the excellent little book just published by Mr. Ingram on the history of the Irish Union (Macmillan) it is said, and said with truth, that the odious penal legislation against Catholics which began some years later was simply the rebound from the much more atrocious acts of this purely Irish Assembly. Macaulay tells us how it was filled with men of native lineage with all its characteristic names. The means taken by them, at once cruel and treacherous, to persecute the rival creed are also authentically set forth in the same brilliant narrative.

Let us abominate both persecutions with equal heartiness, and religious hatred in all its forms. Let us honour and admire the many elements in Irish character which, when mixed with others, may make, and have made, many Irishmen an honour to their country, to our common Empire, and even to the world. Let us try to believe, if we can, that the spirit of pure religious persecution belongs— and belongs only — to the past; but do not let political passion and fanaticism distort history, and by these distortions deprive it of its terrible but blessed lessons for us all.

ARGYLL.

June 3, 1887.

Printed by T. and A. CONSTABLE, Printers to Her Majesty,
at the Edinburgh University Press.

15 A CASTLE STREET,
EDINBURGH, *Jun.* 1888.

LIST OF BOOKS PUBLISHED BY
DAVID DOUGLAS.

————→>∘<←————

View of the Political State of Scotland in the last
Century. A Confidential Report on the Political Opinions, Family Connections, or Personal Circumstances, of the 2662 County Voters in 1788. Edited, with an introductory account of the Law relating to County Elections, by Sir CHARLES ELPHINSTONE ADAM of Blair-Adam, Bart., Barrister-at-Law. Crown 8vo, 5s.

On the Philosophy of Kant.
By ROBERT ADAMSON, M.A., Professor of Logic and Mental Philosophy, Owens College ; formerly Examiner in Philosophy in the University of Edinburgh. Ex. fcap. 8vo, 6s.

The Age of Lead: A Twenty Years' Retrospect.
In three Fyttes. "VAE VICTIS." Second Edition. Sm. crown 8vo, 2s. 6d.

The New Amphion: Being the Book of the Edinburgh
University Union Fancy Fair, in which are contained sundry Artistick, Instructive, and Diverting Matters. *all now made publick for the first time.* 12mo, Illustrated, 5s. ; Large-Paper Edition, 21s. (only 100 Copies printed).

"An especially dainty little morsel for the lovers of choice books."—*Academy.*
"There is no need to say that the book is valuable. It will be eagerly and widely sought for. . . . The external appointments are such as would charm the most fastidious bibliomaniac."—*Scotsman.*

Stories by Thomas Bailey Aldrich.
THE QUEEN OF SHEBA. 1s., or in cloth, gilt top, 2s.
MARJORIE DAW, and other Stories. 1s., or in cloth, gilt top, 2s.
PRUDENCE PALFREY. 1s., or in cloth, gilt top, 2s.
THE STILLWATER TRAGEDY. 2 vols. 2s., or in cloth, gilt top, 4s.

"Mr. Aldrich is, perhaps, entitled to stand at the head of American humourists."—*Athenæum.*
"*Marjorie Daw* is a clever piece of literary work."—*Saturday Review.*

Johnny Gibb of Gushetneuk in the Parish of Pyketillim,
with Glimpses of Parish Politics about A.D. 1843. By WILLIAM ALEXANDER, LL.D. Eighth Edition, with Glossary, Ex. fcap. 8vo, 2s.

Seventh Edition, with Twenty Lithographic Illustrations—Portraits and Landscapes—by GEORGE REID, R.S.A. Demy 8vo, 10s. 6d. Net.

"A most vigorous and truthful delineation of local character, drawn from a portion of the country where that character is peculiarly worthy of careful study and record."—*The Right Hon. W. E. Gladstone.*

Life among my Ain Folk.
By WILLIAM ALEXANDER, LL.D., Author of "Johnny Gibb of Gushetneuk." Ex. fcap. 8vo. Second Edition. Cloth, 2s. 6d. Paper, 2s.

Notes and Sketches of Northern Rural Life in the
Eighteenth Century, by WILLIAM ALEXANDER, LL.D., the Author of "Johnny Gibb of Gushetneuk." Ex. fcap. 8vo, 2s. Cloth, 2s. 6d.

American Authors.

Latest Editions. Revised by the Authors. In 1s. volumes. By Post, 1s. 2d.
Printed by Constable, and published with the sanction of the Authors.

By W. D. HOWELLS.
A FOREGONE CONCLUSION.
A CHANCE ACQUAINTANCE.
THEIR WEDDING JOURNEY.
A COUNTERFEIT PRESENTMENT.
THE LADY OF THE AROOSTOOK. 2 vols.
OUT OF THE QUESTION.
THE UNDISCOVERED COUNTRY. 2 vols.
A FEARFUL RESPONSIBILITY.
VENETIAN LIFE. 2 vols.
ITALIAN JOURNEYS. 2 vols.
THE RISE OF SILAS LAPHAM. 2 vols.
INDIAN SUMMER. 2 vols.

By FRANK R. STOCKTON.
RUDDER GRANGE.
THE LADY OR THE TIGER?
A BORROWED MONTH.

By GEO. W. CURTIS.
PRUE AND I.

By J. C. HARRIS (*Uncle Remus*).
MINGO, AND OTHER SKETCHES.

By GEO. W. CABLE.
OLD CREOLE DAYS.
MADAME DELPHINE.

By B. W. HOWARD.
ONE SUMMER.

By JOHN BURROUGHS.
WINTER SUNSHINE.
PEPACTON.
LOCUSTS AND WILD HONEY.
WAKE-ROBIN.
BIRDS AND POETS.
FRESH FIELDS.

By OLIVER WENDELL HOLMES.
THE AUTOCRAT OF THE BREAKFAST
    TABLE. 2 vols.
THE POET. 2 vols.
THE PROFESSOR. 2 vols.

By G. P. LATHROP.
AN ECHO OF PASSION.

By R. G. WHITE.
MR. WASHINGTON ADAMS.

By T. B. ALDRICH.
THE QUEEN OF SHEBA.
MARJORIE DAW.
PRUDENCE PALFREY.
THE STILLWATER TRAGEDY. 2 vols.

By B. MATTHEWS and H. C. BUNNER.
IN PARTNERSHIP.

By WILLIAM WINTER.
SHAKESPEARE'S ENGLAND.

*** *Other Volumes of this attractive Series in preparation.*
Any of the above may be had bound in Cloth extra, at 2s. each vol.

" A set of charming little books."—*Blackwood's Magazine.*
" A remarkably pretty series."—*Saturday Review.*
"These neat and minute volumes are creditable alike to printer and publisher."
—*Pall Mall Gazette.*
" The most graceful and delicious little volumes with which we are acquainted."
—*Freeman.*
"Soundly and tastefully bound . . . a little model of typography, . . . and the
contents are worthy of the dress."—*St. James's Gazette.*
"The delightful shilling series of ' American Authors' introduced by Mr. David
Douglas has afforded pleasure to thousands of persons."—*Figaro.*
"The type is delightfully legible, and the page is pleasant for the eye to rest
upon ; even in these days of cheap editions we have seen nothing that has pleased
us so well."—*Literary World.*

American Statesmen.

A Series of Biographies of men conspicuous in the Political History of the
United States. Edited by JOHN T. MORSE, Jun.
Small crown 8vo, price 6s. each vol.

1. THOMAS JEFFERSON. By JOHN T. MORSE, Jun.
2. SAMUEL ADAMS. By JAMES K. HOSMER.
    " A man who, in the history of the American Revolution, is second only to
    Washington."
3. ALEXANDER HAMILTON. By HENRY CABOT LODGE.
    With a Preface containing the " Declaration of Independence," " Articles of
    Confederation," and the Constitution of the United States.
4. HENRY CLAY. By CARL SCHURZ. 2 vols., 12s.

Alma Mater's Mirror.

Edited by THOMAS SPENCER BAYNES and LEWIS CAMPBELL, Professors in the
University, St. Andrews. Printed in red and black, on antique paper. Bound
in white, richly tooled in gold in the ancient manner, with ribbon fastening. In
box, Price 5s.

Modern Horsemanship. A New Method of Teaching

Riding and Training by means of pictures from the life. By E. L. ANDERSON. New and Revised Edition, containing some observations upon the mode of changing lead in the Gallop. Illustrated by 28 Instantaneous Photographs. Demy 8vo. 21s.

Vice in the Horse and other Papers on Horses and

Riding. By E. L. ANDERSON, Author of "Modern Horsemanship." Illustrated. Demy 8vo, 5s.

The Gallop.

By E. L. ANDERSON. Illustrated by Instantaneous Photography. Fcap. 4to, 2s. 6d.

Scotland in Early Christian Times.

By JOSEPH ANDERSON, LL.D., Keeper of the National Museum of the Antiquaries of Scotland. (Being the Rhind Lectures in Archæology for 1879 and 1880.) 2 vols. Demy 8vo, profusely Illustrated. 12s. each volume.

Contents of Vol. I.—Celtic Churches—Monasteries—Hermitages—Round Towers —Illuminated Manuscripts—Bells—Crosiers—Reliquaries, etc.

Contents of Vol. II.—Celtic Medal-Work and Sculptured Monuments, their Art and Symbolism—Inscribed Monuments in Runics and Oghams—Bilingual inscriptions, etc.

Scotland in Pagan Times.

By JOSEPH ANDERSON, LL.D. (Being the Rhind Lectures in Archæology for 1881 and 1882.) In 2 vols. Demy 8vo, profusely Illustrated. 12s. each volume.

Contents of Vol. I.—THE IRON AGE.—Viking Burials and Hoards of Silver and Ornaments—Arms, Dress, etc., of the Viking Time—Celtic Art of the Pagan Period—Decorated Mirrors—Enamelled Armlets—Architecture and Contents of the Brochs—Lake-Dwellings—Earth Houses, etc.

Contents of Vol. II.—THE BRONZE AND STONE AGES.—Cairn Burial of the Bronze Age and Cremation Cemeteries—Urns of Bronze-Age Types—Stone Circles— Stone Settings—Gold Ornaments—Implements and Weapons of Bronze—Cairn Burial of the Stone Age—Chambered Cairns—Urns of Stone-Age Types—Implements and Weapons of Stone.

Scotland as it was and as it is.

By the DUKE OF ARGYLL. 1 vol. Demy 8vo. Illustrated. New Edition. Carefully Revised. 7s. 6d.

Contents.—Celtic Feudalism—The Age of Charters—The Age of Covenants— The Epoch of the Clans—The Appeal from Chiefs to Owners—The Response to the Appeal—Before the Dawn—The Burst of Industry—The Fruits of Mind.

"Infinitely superior as regards the Highland land question to any statement yet made by the other side."—*Scotsman.*

" It presents a series of strikingly picturesque sketches of the wild society and rude manners of the olden time."—*Times.*

Crofts and Farms in the Hebrides:

Being an account of the Management of an Island Estate for 130 Years. By the DUKE OF ARGYLL. Demy 8vo, 83 pages, 1s.

Continuity and Catastrophes in Geology.

An Address to the Edinburgh Geological Society on its Fiftieth Anniversary, 1st November 1883. By the DUKE OF ARGYLL. Demy 8vo, 1s.

The History of Liddesdale, Eskdale, Ewesdale, Wauch-

opedale, and the Debateable Land. Part I. from the Twelfth Century to 1530. By ROBERT BRUCE ARMSTRONG. The edition is limited to 275 copies demy quarto , and 105 copies on large paper (10 inches by 13). 42s. and 84s.

Morning Clouds:

Being divers Poems by H. B. BAILDON, B.A. Cantab., Author of "Rosamund etc. Ex. fcap. 8vo, 5s.

By the same Author.

First Fruits. 5s.   **Rosamund. 5s.**

Reminiscences of Golf on St. Andrews Links.
By JAMES BALFOUR. Price 1s.

On Both Sides. By FRANCES C. BAYLOR. 1 vol. 6s.

Dr. Heidenhoff's Process.
By EDWARD BELLAMY. Crown 8vo, 6s.

Miss Ludington's Sister: a Romance of Immortality.
By EDWARD BELLAMY, Author of "Dr. Heidenhoff's Process." Crown 8vo, 6s.

Bible Readings. Extra fcap. 8vo, 2s.

The Voyage of the Paper Canoe.
A Geographical Journey of 2500 miles, from Quebec to the Gulf of Mexico, during the year 1874-75. By N. H. BISHOP. With Maps and Plates. Demy 8vo, 10s. 6d.

On Self-Culture:
Intellectual, Physical, and Moral. A *Vade-Mecum* for Young Men and Students. By JOHN STUART BLACKIE, Emeritus Professor of Greek in the University of Edinburgh. Sixteenth Edition. Fcap. 8vo, 2s. 6d.

"Every parent should put it into the hands of his son."—*Scotsman.*

"Students in all countries would do well to take as their *vade-mecum* a little book on self-culture by the eminent Professor of Greek in the University of Edinburgh."—*Medical Press and Circular.*

"An invaluable manual to be put into the hands of students and young men." —*Era.*

"Written in that lucid and nervous prose of which he is a master."—*Spectator.*

"An adequate guide to a generous, eager, and sensible life."—*Academy.*

"The volume is a little thing, but it is a *multum in parvo*, . . . a little locket gemmed within and without with real stones fitly set."—*Courant.*

By the same Author.

On Greek Pronunciation. Demy 8vo, 3s. 6d.

On Beauty.
Crown 8vo, cloth, 8s. 6d.

Lyrical Poems.
Crown 8vo, cloth, 7s. 6d.

The Language and Literature of the Scottish Highlands. Crown 8vo, 6s.

Four Phases of Morals:
Socrates, Aristotle, Christianity, and Utilitarianism. Lectures delivered before the Royal Institution, London. Ex. fcap. 8vo, Second Edition, 5s.

Songs of Religion and Life. Fcap. 8vo, 6s.

Musa Burschicosa.
A book of Songs for Students and University Men. Fcap. 8vo, 2s. 6d.

War Songs of the Germans. Fcap. 8vo, 2s. 6d. cloth ; 2s. paper.

Political Tracts. No. 1. GOVERNMENT. No. 2. EDUCATION. 1s. each.

Gaelic Societies. Highland Depopulation and Land Law Reform. Demy 8vo, 6d.

Homer and the Iliad. In three Parts. 4 vols. Demy 8vo, 42s.

Love Revealed: Meditations on the Parting Words of
Jesus with His Disciples, in John xiii-xvii. By the Rev. GEORGE BOWEN, Missionary at Bombay. New Edition. Small 4to, 5s.

"No true Christian could put the book down without finding in himself some traces of the blessed unction which drops from every page."—*Record.*

"Here is a feast of fat things, of fat things full of marrow."—*Sword and Trowel.*

"A more stimulating work of its class has not appeared for many a long day." —*Scotsman.*

"The present work is eminently qualified to help the devotional life."—*Literary World.*

"He writes plainly and earnestly, and with a true appreciation of the tender beauties of what are really among the finest passages in the New Testament."— *Glasgow Herald.*

"Verily, Verily," The Amens of Christ.

By the Rev. GEORGE BOWEN, Missionary at Bombay. Small 4to, cloth, 5s.
"For private and devotional reading this book will be found very helpful and stimulative."—*Literary World.*

Daily Meditations by Rev. George Bowen, Missionary

at Bombay. With Introductory Notice by Rev. W. HANNA, D.D., Author of "The Last Day of our Lord's Passion." New Edition. Small 4to, cloth, 5s.
"These meditations are the production of a missionary whose mental history is very remarkable. . . . His conversion to a religious life is undoubtedly one of the most remarkable on record. They are all distinguished by a tone of true piety, and are wholly free from a sectarian or controversial bias."—*Morning Post.*

Works by John Brown, M.D., F.R.S.E.

HORÆ SUBSECIVÆ. 3 Vols. 22s. 6d.
Vol. I. Locke and Sydenham. Fifth Edition, with Portrait by James Faed. Crown 8vo, 7s. 6d.
Vol. II. Rab and his Friends. Thirteenth Edition. Crown 8vo, 7s. 6d.
Vol. III. John Leech. Fifth Edition, with Portrait by George Reid, R.S.A. Crown 8vo, 7s. 6d.

Separate Papers, extracted from "Horæ Subsecivæ."

RAB AND HIS FRIENDS. With India-proof Portrait of the Author after Faed, and seven Illustrations after Sir G. Harvey, Sir Noel Paton, Mrs. Blackburn, and G. Reid, R.S.A. Demy 4to, cloth, 9s.
MARJORIE FLEMING : A Sketch. Being a Paper entitled "Pet Marjorie ; A Story of a Child's Life fifty years ago." New Edition, with Illustrations. Demy 4to, 7s. 6d. and 6s.
RAB AND HIS FRIENDS. Cheap Illustrated Edition. Square 12mo, ornamental wrapper, 1s.
LETTER TO THE REV. JOHN CAIRNS, D.D. Second Edition, crown 8vo, sewed, 2s.
ARTHUR H. HALLAM. Fcap., sewed, 2s. ; cloth, 2s. 6d.
RAB AND HIS FRIENDS. Sixty-sixth thousand. Fcap., sewed, 6d.
MARJORIE FLEMING : A Sketch. Sixteenth Thousand. Fcap., sewed, 6d.
OUR DOGS. Twentieth thousand. Fcap., sewed, 6d.
"WITH BRAINS, SIR." Seventh thousand. Fcap., sewed, 6d.
MINCHMOOR. Tenth Thousand. Fcap., sewed, 6d.
JEEMS THE DOOR-KEEPER : A Lay Sermon. Twelfth thousand. Price 6d.
THE ENTERKIN. Seventh Thousand. Price 6d.
PLAIN WORDS ON HEALTH. Twenty-seventh thousand. Price 6d.
SOMETHING ABOUT A WELL : WITH MORE OF OUR DOGS. Price 6d.

From Schola to Cathedral. A Study of Early Christian

Architecture in its relation to the life of the Church. By G. BALDWIN-BROWN, Professor of Fine Art in the University of Edinburgh. Demy 8vo, Illustrated, 7s. 6d.
The book treats of the beginnings of Christian Architecture, from the point of view of recent discoveries and theories, with a special reference to the outward resemblance of early Christian communities to other religious associations of the time.

The Capercaillie in Scotland.

By J. A. HARVIE-BROWN. Etchings on Copper, and Map illustrating the extension of its range since its Restoration at Taymouth in 1837 and 1838. Demy 8vo, 8s. 6d.

A Vertebrate Fauna of Sutherland, Caithness, and

West Cromarty. By J. A. HARVIE-BROWN, F.R.S.E., F.Z.S., Vice-President Royal Physical Society, Edinburgh ; Member of the British Ornithologists' Union, etc., and T. E. BUCKLEY, B.A., F.Z.S., Member of the British Ornithologists' Union, etc. Small 4to, with Map and Plates. 30s.

The History of Selkirkshire ; Chronicles of Ettrick Forest.

By T. CRAIG-BROWN. Two vols. Demy 4to, Illustrated. £4, 10s. Net.

Pugin Studentship Drawings. Being a selection from

Sketches, Measured Drawings, and details of Domestic and Ecclesiastic Buildings in England and Scotland. By G. WASHINGTON-BROWNE, F.S.A. Scot., Architect. 1 vol. Folio, Illustrated, 45s.

"The Red Book of Menteith" Reviewed.

By GEORGE BURNETT, Advocate, Lyon King of Arms. Small 4to, 5s.

Next Door. A Novel. By CLARE LOUISE BURNHAM. Crown 8vo,

7s. 6d.

"A strangely interesting story."—*St. James's Gazette.*

John Burroughs's Essays.

Six Books of Nature, Animal Life, and Literature. Choice Edition. Revised by
the Author. 6 vols., cloth, 12s.; or in smooth ornamental wrappers, 6s.; or
separately at 1s. each vol., or 2s. in cloth.

WINTER SUNSHINE.	FRESH FIELDS.
LOCUSTS AND WILD HONEY.	BIRDS AND POETS.
WAKE-ROBIN.	PEPACTON.

"Whichever essay I read, I am glad I read it, for pleasanter reading, to those
who love the country, with all its enchanting sights and sounds, cannot be im-
agined."—*Spectator.*

"Mr. Burroughs is one of the most delightful of American Essayists, steeped in
culture to the finger-ends."—*Pall Mall Gazette.*

FRESH FIELDS. By JOHN BURROUGHS. Library Edition. Crown 8vo, 6s.
SIGNS AND SEASONS. Library Edition. Crown 8vo, 6s.

Dr. Sevier: A Novel.

By GEO. W. CABLE, Author of "Old Creole Days," etc. In 2 vols., crown 8vo,
price 12s.

Old Creole Days.

By GEO. W. CABLE. 1s.; and in Cloth, 2s.

"We cannot recall any contemporary American writer of fiction who possesses
some of the best gifts of the novelist in a higher degree."—*St. James's Gazette.*

Madame Delphine.

By GEO. W. CABLE, Author of "Old Creole Days." 1s.; and in cloth, 2s.

Contents.—Madame Delphine—Carancro—Grande Pointe.

Memoir of John Brown, D.D.

By JOHN CAIRNS, D.D., Berwick-on-Tweed. Crown 8vo, 7s. 6d.

My Indian Journal.

Containing Descriptions of the principal Field Sports of India, with Notes on the
Natural History and Habits of the Wild Animals of the Country. By Colonel
WALTER CAMPBELL, Author of "The Old Forest Ranger." Small demy 8vo, with
Illustrations by Wolf, 16s.

Life and Works of Rev. Thomas Chalmers, D.D., LL.D.

MEMOIRS OF THE REV. THOMAS CHALMERS. By Rev. W. HANNA, D.D., LL.D. New
Edition. 2 vols. crown 8vo, cloth, 12s.
DAILY SCRIPTURE READINGS. Cheap Edition. 2 vols. crown 8vo, 10s.
ASTRONOMICAL DISCOURSES, 1s.
COMMERCIAL DISCOURSES, 1s.
SELECT WORKS, in 12 vols., crown 8vo, cloth, per vol. 6s.

Lectures on the Romans. 2 vols.
Sermons. 2 vols.
Natural Theology, Lectures on Butler's Analogy, etc. 1 vol.
Christian Evidences, Lectures on Paley's Evidences, etc. 1 vol.
Institutes of Theology. 2 vols.
Political Economy, with Cognate Essays. 1 vol.
Polity of a Nation. 1 vol.
Church and College Establishments. 1 vol.
Moral Philosophy, Introductory Essays, Index, etc. 1 vol.

Lectures on Surgical Anatomy.

By JOHN CHIENE, M.D., Professor of Surgery in the University of Edinburgh. In demy 8vo. With numerous Illustrations drawn on Stone by BERJEAU. 12s. 6d.

"The book will be a great help to both teachers and taught, and students can depend upon the teaching as being sound."—*Medical Times and Gazette.*

Lectures on the Elements or First Principles of Surgery.

By JOHN CHIENE, M.D., Professor of Surgery in the University of Edinburgh. Demy 8vo, 2s. 6d.

The Odes of Horace.

Translated by T. RUTHERFURD CLARK, Advocate. 16mo, 6s.

Scala Naturæ, and other Poems.

By JOHN CLELAND. Fcap. 8vo, 5s.

An Examination of the Trials which have hitherto

occurred in Scotland for Sedition—1793 to 1849. By the late LORD COCKBURN. 2 vols. demy 8vo.   [*In the Press.*

Circuit Journeys from 1837 to 1854.

By the late LORD COCKBURN. 1 vol. crown 8vo.   [*In the Press.*

Archibald Constable and his Literary Correspondents:

a Memorial. By his Son, THOMAS CONSTABLE. 3 vols. demy 8vo, 36s., with Portrait.

"He (Mr. Constable) was a genius in the publishing world. . . . The creator of the Scottish publishing trade."—*Times.*

The Earldom of Mar, in Sunshine and in Shade, during

Five Hundred Years. With incidental Notices of the leading Cases of Scottish Dignities from the reign of King Charles I. till now. By ALEXANDER, EARL OF CRAWFORD AND BALCARRES, LORD LINDSAY, etc. etc. 2 vols. demy 8vo, 32s.

The Crime of Henry Vane: a Study with a Moral.

By J. S. of Dale, Author of "Guerndale." Crown 8vo, 6s.

A Clinical and Experimental Study of the Bladder

during Parturition. By J. H. CROOM, M.B., F.R.C.P.E. Small 4to, with Illustrations, 6s.

Wild Men and Wild Beasts.

Adventures in Camp and Jungle. By Lieut.-Colonel GORDON CUMMING. With Illustrations by Lieut.-Colonel BAIGRIE and others. Small 4to, 24s.

Also a cheaper edition, with *Lithographic* Illustrations. 8vo, 12s.

Prue and I.

By GEORGE WILLIAM CURTIS. 1s. paper ; or 2s. cloth extra.

Contents.—Dinner Time—My Chateaux—Sea from Shore—Titbottom's Spectacles—A Cruise in the Flying Dutchman—Family Portraits—Our Cousin the Curate.

"This is a dainty piece of work, and well deserved reprinting."—*Athenæum.*

"These charming sketches will be enjoyed by all cultured readers."—*Daily Chronicle.*

The Story of Burnt Njal; or, Life in Iceland at the end

of the Tenth Century. From the Icelandic of the Njals Saga. By Sir GEORGE WEBBE DASENT, D.C.L. 2 vols. demy 8vo, with Maps and Plans, 28s.

Gisli the Outlaw.

From the Icelandic. By Sir GEORGE WEBBE DASENT, D.C.L. Small 4to, with Illustrations, 7s. 6d.

A Daughter of the Philistines: A Novel.

Crown 8vo, 6s. Also a cheaper edition in paper binding, 2s.

"The story is very powerfully told, possesses a piquantly satirical flavour, and possesses the very real attraction of freshness."—*Scotsman.*

"It is cleverly and brightly written."—*Academy.*

A Manual of Chemical Analysis.

By Professor WILLIAM DITTMAR. Ex. fcap. 8vo, 5s.
TABLES FORMING AN APPENDIX TO DITTO. Demy 8vo, 3s. 6d.

A Chat in the Saddle; or Patroclus and Penelope.

By THEO. A. DODGE, Lieut.-Colonel, United States Army. Illustrated by 14 Instantaneous Photographs. Demy 8vo, half-leather binding, 21s.

The Fireside Tragedy, etc.

By Sir GEORGE DOUGLAS, Bart. Fcap. 8vo, 5s.

Veterinary Medicines; their Actions and Uses.

By FINLAY DUN. Sixth Edition, revised and enlarged. Demy 8vo, 15s.

Social Life in Former Days;

Chiefly in the Province of Moray. Illustrated by Letters and Family Papers. By E. DUNBAR DUNBAR, late Captain 21st Fusiliers. 2 vols. Demy 8vo, 19s. 6d.

Letters of Thomas Erskine of Linlathen.

Edited by WILLIAM HANNA, D.D., Author of the "Memoirs of Dr. Chalmers," etc. Fourth Edition. Crown 8vo, 7s. 6d.

The Unconditional Freeness of the Gospel.

By THOMAS ERSKINE of Linlathen. New Edition, revised. Crown 8vo, 3s. 6d.

By the same Author.

The Brazen Serpent:

Or, Life coming through Death. Third Edition. Crown 8vo, 5s.

The Internal Evidence of Revealed Religion.

Crown 8vo, 5s.

The Spiritual Order,

And other Papers selected from the MSS. of the late THOMAS ERSKINE of Linlathen. Third Edition. Crown 8vo, 5s.

The Doctrine of Election,

And its Connection with the General Tenor of Christianity, illustrated especially from the Epistle to the Romans. Second Edition. Crown 8vo, 6s.

Three Visits to America.

By EMILY FAITHFULL. Demy 8vo, 9s.

Ogham Inscriptions in Ireland, Wales, and Scotland.

By the late SIR SAMUEL FERGUSON, President of the Royal Irish Academy, Deputy Keeper of the Public Records of Ireland, LL.D., Queen's Counsel, etc. (Being the Rhind Lectures in Archæology for 1884.) 1 vol. demy 8vo, 12s.

Twelve Sketches of Scenery and Antiquities on the

Line of the Great North of Scotland Railway. By GEORGE REID, R.S.A. With Illustrative Letterpress by W. FERGUSON of Kinmundy. 4to, 15s.

Guide to the Great North of Scotland Railway.

By W. FERGUSON of Kinmundy. Crown 8vo; in paper cover, 1s.; cloth cover, 1s. 6d.

Robert Ferguson "The Plotter," or, The Secret of the

Rye House Conspiracy and the Story of a Strange Career. By JAMES FERGUSON, Advocate. A Biography of one of the strangest figures of English Politics in the period between the Restoration and the Accession of the House of Hanover. Demy 8vo, 15s.

Letters and Journals of Mrs. Calderwood of Polton,

from England, Holland, and the Low Countries, in 1756. Edited by ALEX. FERGUSSON, Lieut.-Colonel, Author of "Henry Erskine and his Kinsfolk." Demy 8vo, Illustrated, 18s.

The Laird of Lag; A Life-Sketch of Sir Robert Grierson.
By ALEX. FERGUSSON, Lieut.-Colonel, Author of "Mrs. Calderwood's Journey." Demy 8vo, with Illustrations, 12s.

Autobiography of Mrs. Fletcher
(of Edinburgh), with Letters and other Family Memorials. Edited by her Daughter. Third Edition. Crown 8vo, 7s. 6d.

L'Histoire de France.
Par M. LAME FLEURY. New Edition, corrected to 1883. 19mo, cloth, 2s. 6d.

The Deepening of the Spiritual Life.
By A. P. FORBES, D.C.L., Bishop of Brechin. Seventh Edition. Paper, 1s.; cloth, 1s. 6d. Calf, red edges, 3s. 6d.

Kalendars of Scottish Saints,
With Personal Notices of those of Alba, etc. By ALEXANDER PENROSE FORBES, D.C.L., Bishop of Brechin. 4to, price £3, 3s. A few copies for sale on large paper, £5, 15s. 6d.

"A truly valuable contribution to the archæology of Scotland."—*Guardian.*

"We must not forget to thank the author for the great amount of information he has put together, and for the labour he has bestowed on a work which can never be remunerative."—*Saturday Review.*

Missale Drummondiense. The Ancient Irish Missal in
the possession of the Baroness Willoughby d'Eresby. Edited by the Rev. G. H. FORBES. Half-Morocco, Demy 8vo, 12s.

Forestry and Forest Products.
Prize Essays of the Edinburgh International Forestry Exhibition 1884. Edited by JOHN RATTRAY M.A., B.Sc., and HUGH ROBERT MILL, D.Sc. Demy 8vo, Illustrated, 9s.

Fragments of Truth:
Being the Exposition of several Passages of Scripture. Third Edition. Ex. fcap. 8vo, 5s.

Studies in English History.
By JAMES GAIRDNER and JAMES SPEDDING. Demy 8vo, 12s.
Contents.—The Lollards—Sir John Falstaff—Katherine of Arragon's First and Second Marriages—Case of Sir Thomas Overbury—Divine Right of Kings—Sunday, Ancient and Modern.

Industrial Exhibitions and Modern Progress.
By PATRICK GEDDES. Fcap. 8vo, 1s.

Gifts for Men.
By X. H. Crown 8vo, 6s.
"There is hardly a living theologian who might not be proud to claim many of her thoughts as his own."—*Glasgow Herald.*

Sketches, Literary and Theological:
Being Selections from the unpublished MSS. of the Rev. GEORGE GILFILLAN. Edited by FRANK HENDERSON, Esq., M.P. Demy 8vo, 7s. 6d.

The Roof of the World:
Being the Narrative of a Journey over the High Plateau of Tibet to the Russian Frontier, and the Oxus Sources on Pamir. By Brigadier-General T. E. GORDON, C.S.I. With numerous Illustrations. Royal 8vo, 31s. 6d.

Ladies' Old-Fashioned Shoes.
By T. WATSON GREIG, of Glencarse. Folio, illustrated by 11 Chromolithographs. 31s. 6d.

Mingo, and other Sketches in Black and White.
By JOEL CHANDLER HARRIS (*Uncle Remus*). 1s.; and in cloth, 2s.

Works by Margaret Maria Gordon (née Brewster).

THE HOME LIFE OF SIR DAVID BREWSTER. By his Daughter. Second Edition. Crown 8vo, 6s. Also a cheaper Edition. Crown 8vo, 2s. 6d.

WORK; Or, Plenty to do and How to do it. Thirty-Sixth Thousand. Fcap. 8vo, cloth, 2s. 6d.

WORKERS. Fourth Thousand. Fcap. 8vo, limp cloth, 1s.

LITTLE MILLIE AND HER FOUR PLACES. Cheap Edition. Fifty-ninth Thousand. Limp cloth, 1s.

SUNBEAMS IN THE COTTAGE; Or, What Women may Do. A Narrative chiefly addressed to the Working Classes. Cheap Edition. Forty-fifth Thousand. Limp cloth, 1s.

PREVENTION; or, An Appeal to Economy and Common Sense. 8vo, 6d.

THE WORD AND THE WORLD. Twelfth Edition. 2d.

LEAVES OF HEALING FOR THE SICK AND SORROWFUL. Cheap Edition, limp cloth, 2s.

THE MOTHERLESS BOY. With an Illustration by Sir NOEL PATON, R.S.A. Cheap Edition, limp cloth, 1s.

OUR DAUGHTERS; An Account of the Young Women's Christian Association and Institute Union. 2d.

HAY MACDOWALL GRANT OF ARNDILLY; His Life, Labours, and Teaching. New and Cheaper Edition. 1 vol. crown 8vo, limp cloth, 2s. 6d.

The Life of our Lord.

By the Rev. WILLIAM HANNA, D.D., LL.D. 6 vols., handsomely bound in cloth extra, gilt edges, 30s.

Separate vols., cloth extra, gilt edges, 5s. each.

1. THE EARLIER YEARS OF OUR LORD. Fifth Edition.
2. THE MINISTRY IN GALILEE. Fourth Edition.
3. THE CLOSE OF THE MINISTRY. Sixth Thousand.
4. THE PASSION WEEK. Sixth Thousand.
5. THE LAST DAY OF OUR LORD'S PASSION. Twenty-third Edition.
6. THE FORTY DAYS AFTER THE RESURRECTION. Eighth Edition.

The Resurrection of the Dead.

By WILLIAM HANNA, D.D., LL.D. Second Edition. Fcap. 8vo, 5s.

Notes of Caithness Family History.

By the late JOHN HENDERSON, W.S. 4to, in cloth, 21s.

The High Estate of Service.

Fcap. 8vo, 1s.

Errors in the Use of English.

Illustrated from the Writings of English Authors, from the Fourteenth Century to our own Time. By the late W. B. HODGSON, LL.D., Professor of Political Economy in the University of Edinburgh. Fifth Edition. Crown 8vo, 3s. 6d.

"Those who most need such a book as Dr. Hodgson's will probably be the last to look into it. It will certainly amuse its readers, and will probably teach them a good deal which they did not know, or at least never thought about, before."— *Saturday Review.*

"His conversation, as every one who had the pleasure of his acquaintance knows, sparkled with anecdote and epigram, and not a little of the lustre and charm of his talk shines out of those pages."—*The Scotsman.*

Life and Letters of W. B. Hodgson, LL.D., late Professor of Political Economy in the University of Edinburgh. Edited by Professor J. M. D. MEIKLEJOHN, M.A. Crown 8vo, 7s. 6d.

Sketches: Personal and Pensive.

By WILLIAM HODGSON. Fcap. 8vo, 2s. 6d.

"Quasi Cursores." Portraits of the High Officers and

Professors of the University of Edinburgh. Drawn and Etched by WILLIAM HOLE, A.R.S.A. The book is printed on beautiful hand-made paper by Messrs. T. & A. Constable. It contains 45 Plates (64 Portraits), with Biographical Notices of all the present Incumbents. The impression is strictly limited. Quarto Edition (750 Copies only for sale), £2, 10s. Folio Edition, Japan Proofs (100 Copies only for sale), £5, 10s.

Memorial Catalogue of the French and Dutch Loan

Collection, Edinburgh International Exhibition. Letterpress by W. E. HENLEY. Etchings and Sketches by WILLIAM HOLE, A.R.S.A., and PHILIP ZILCKEN. The book is printed by CONSTABLE on wove handmade paper, in dark-green ink. It gives an account of the rise of Romanticism, a biography of the principal Masters of that School, and a description of each of the Pictures. It is illustrated by fifteen original Etchings and fifty-four outline Sketches. Pott folio. Edition limited to 520 Copies. £3, 3s.

The Breakfast Table Series.

In 6 vols. By OLIVER WENDELL HOLMES. New and Revised Editions, containing Prefaces and additional Bibliographical Notes by the Author.

THE AUTOCRAT OF THE BREAKFAST TABLE. 2 vols., 2s.
THE POET AT THE BREAKFAST TABLE. 2 vols., 2s.
THE PROFESSOR AT THE BREAKFAST TABLE. 2 vols., 2s.

    Also bound in dark blue cloth, at 2s. a vol., or in a neat cloth box, 15s.

    "Small enough to be carried in any sensibly constructed pocket, clear enough in type to accommodate any fastidious eyesight, pleasant and instructive enough for its perusal to be undertaken with the certainty of present enjoyment and the prospect of future profit."—*Whitehall Review.*

    Also a LIBRARY EDITION, in 3 vols. crown 8vo, printed at the Riverside Press, Cambridge, with a Steel Portrait of the Author, 10s. 6d. each volume.

    A COMPLETE EDITION of the Poems of OLIVER WENDELL HOLMES, revised by the Author, in 3 vols. [*In the Press.*

Traces in Scotland of Ancient Water Lines, Marine,

Lacustrine, and Fluviatile. By DAVID MILNE-HOME, LL.D., F.R.S.E. Demy 8vo, 3s. 6d.

A Sketch of the Life of George Hope of Fenton Barns.

Compiled by his DAUGHTER. Crown 8vo, 6s.

One Summer. By BLANCHE WILLIS HOWARD. Paper, 1s. ; cloth, 1s. 6d. and 2s.

W. D. Howells's Writings :—

In "American Author" Series.

INDIAN SUMMER. 2 vols., 2s.
THE RISE OF SILAS LAPHAM. 2 vols., 2s.
A FOREGONE CONCLUSION. 1 vol., 1s.
A CHANCE ACQUAINTANCE. 1 vol., 1s.
THEIR WEDDING JOURNEY. 1 vol., 1s.
A COUNTERFEIT PRESENTMENT, and THE PARLOUR CAR. 1 vol., 1s.
THE LADY OF THE AROOSTOOK. 2 vols., 2s.
OUT OF THE QUESTION, and AT THE SIGN OF THE SAVAGE. 1 vol. 1s.
THE UNDISCOVERED COUNTRY. 2 vols., 2s.
A FEARFUL RESPONSIBILITY, and TONELLI'S MARRIAGE. 1 vol., 1s.
VENETIAN LIFE. 2 vols., 2s.
ITALIAN JOURNEYS. 2 vols., 2s.
    All the above may be had in cloth at 2s. each vol.

Copyright Library Edition.

A MODERN INSTANCE. 2 vols., 12s.
A WOMAN'S REASON. 2 vols., 12s.
DR. BREEN'S PRACTICE. 1 vol., 3s. 6d.
INDIAN SUMMER. 1 vol., 6s.
APRIL HOPES. 1 vol., 6s.
THE MINISTER'S CHARGE ; OR, THE APPRENTICESHIP OF LEMUEL BARKER. 1 vol., 6s.
TUSCAN CITIES : WITH ILLUSTRATIONS FROM DRAWINGS AND ETCHINGS OF JOSEPH PENNELL and others. 4to, 16s.
MODERN ITALIAN POETS. 1 vol. 7s. 6d.

A Memorial Sketch, and a Selection from the Letters
of the late Lieut. JOHN IRVING, R.N., of H.M.S. "Terror," in Sir John Franklin's Expedition to the Arctic Regions. Edited by BENJAMIN BELL, F.R.C.S.E. With Facsimiles of the Record and Irving's Medal and Map. Post 8vo, 5s.

Jack and Mrs. Brown, and other Stories.
By the Author of "Blindpits." Crown 8vo, paper, 2s. 6d. ; cloth, 3s. 6d.

Zeph : A Posthumous Story.
By HELEN JACKSON ("H.H."). Author of "Ramona," etc. Crown 8vo, 6s.

Epitaphs and Inscriptions from Burial-Grounds and
Old Buildings in the North-East of Scotland. By the late ANDREW JERVISE, F.S.A. Scot. With a Memoir of the Author. Vol. II. Cloth, small 4to, 32s.
Do.   do.   Roxburghe Edition, 42s.

The History and Traditions of the Land of the Lindsays
in Angus and Mearns. By the late ANDREW JERVISE, F.S.A. Scot. New Edition, Edited and Revised by the Rev. JAMES GAMMACK, M.A. Demy 8vo, 14s.
Large Paper, demy 4to, 42s.

Memorials of Angus and the Mearns : an Account,
Historical, Antiquarian, and Traditionary, of the Castles and Towns visited by Edward I., and of the Barons, Clergy, and others who swore Fealty to England in 1291-6. By the late ANDREW JERVISE, F.S.A. Scot. Rewritten and corrected by the Rev. JAMES GAMMACK, M.A. Illustrated with Etchings by W. HOLE, A.R.S.A. 2 vols. Demy 8vo, 28s. ; Large Paper, 2 vols. Demy 4to, 63s.

Sermons by the Rev. John Ker, D.D., Glasgow.
Thirteenth Edition. Crown 8vo, 6s.

Sermons : Second Series : by the Rev. John Ker, D.D.
Second Edition. Crown 8vo, 6s.

Thoughts for Heart and Life.
By the Rev. JOHN KER, D.D. Edited by the Rev. A. L. SIMPSON, D.D., Derby. With Portrait by JAMES FAED. Ex. fcap. 8vo, 4s. 6d.

Memories of Coleorton : Being Letters from Coleridge,
Wordsworth and his Sister, Southey and Sir Walter Scott, to Sir George and Lady Beaumont of Coleorton, Leicestershire. 1803 to 1833. Edited, with Notes and Introduction, by WILLIAM KNIGHT, St. Andrews. 2 vols. crown 8vo, 15s.

The English Lake District as interpreted in the Poems
of Wordsworth. By WILLIAM KNIGHT, Professor of Moral Philosophy in the University of St. Andrews. Ex. fcap. 8vo, 5s.

Colloquia Peripatetica (Deep Sea Soundings):
Being Notes of Conversations with the late John Duncan, LL.D., Professor of Hebrew in the New College, Edinburgh. By WILLIAM KNIGHT, Professor of Moral Philosophy in the University of St. Andrews. Fifth Edition, enlarged, 5s.

Lindores Abbey, and the Burgh of Newburgh ;
Their History and Annals. By ALEXANDER LAING, LL.D., F.S.A. Scot. Small 4to. With Index, and thirteen Full-page and ten Woodcut Illustrations, 21s.

"This is a charming volume in every respect."—*Notes and Queries.*
"The prominent characteristics of the work are its exhaustiveness and the thoroughly philosophic spirit in which it is written."—*Scotsman.*

Recollections of Curious Characters and Pleasant
Places. By CHARLES LANMAN, Washington ; Author of "Adventures in the Wilds of America," "A Canoe Voyage up the Mississippi," "A Tour to the River Saguenay," etc. etc. Small Demy 8vo, 12s.

Essays and Reviews.
By the late HENRY H. LANCASTER, Advocate ; with a Prefatory Notice by the Rev. B. JOWETT, Master of Balliol College, Oxford. Demy 8vo, with Portrait, 14s.

An Echo of Passion.
By GEO. PARSONS LATHROP. 1s. ; and in cloth, 2s.

On the Philosophy of Ethics. An Analytical Essay.
By S. S. LAURIE, A.M., F.R.S.E., Professor of the Theory, History, and Practice of Education in the University of Edinburgh. Demy 8vo, 6s.

Notes on British Theories of Morals.
By Prof. S. S. LAURIE. Demy 8vo, 6s.

Sermons by the Rev. Adam Lind, M.A., Elgin.
Ex. fcap. 8vo, 5s.

Only an Incident.
A Novel. By Miss G. D. LITCHFIELD. Crown 8vo, 6s.

Leaves from the Buik of the West Kirke.
By GEO. LORIMER. With a Preface by the Rev. JAS. MACGREGOR, D.D. 4to.

A Lost Battle. A Novel. 2 vols. Crown 8vo, 17s.
" This in every way remarkable novel."— *Morning Post.*
" We are all the more ready to do justice to the excellence of the author's drawing of characters."—*Athenæum.*

John Calvin, a Fragment by the late Thomas M'Crie,
Author of " The Life of John Knox." Demy 8vo, 6s.

The Parish of Taxwood, and some of its Older Memories.
By Rev. J. R. MACDUFF, D.D. Extra fcap. 8vo, illustrated, 3s. 6d.

Principles of the Algebra of Logic, with Examples.
By ALEX. MACFARLANE, M.A., D.Sc. (Edin.), F.R.S.E. 5s.

The Castellated and Domestic Architecture of Scot-
land, from the Twelfth to the Eighteenth Century. By DAVID M'GIBBON and THOMAS ROSS, Architects. 2 vols., with about 1000 Illustrations of Ground Plans, Sections, Views, Elevations, and Details. Royal 8vo. 42s. each vol. Net.
" No one acquainted with the history of Great Britain can take up this neatly-bound volume . . . without being at once struck by its careful completeness and extreme archæological interest, while all students of architectural style will welcome the work specially for its technical thoroughness."—*Building News.*
" A learned, painstaking, and highly important work."—*Scottish Review.*
" One of the most important and complete books on Scottish architecture that has ever been compiled."—*Scotsman.*
" The authors merit the thanks of all architectural readers."—*Builder.*

Memoir of Sir James Dalrymple, First Viscount Stair.
A Study in the History of Scotland and Scotch Law during the Seventeenth Century. By Æ. J. G. MACKAY, Advocate. 8vo, 12s.

Storms and Sunshine of a Soldier's Life.
Lt.-General COLIN MACKENZIE, C.B., 1825-1881. With a Portrait. 2 vols. Crown 8vo, 15s.
" A very readable biography . . . of one of the bravest and ablest officers of the East India Company's army."—*Saturday Review.*

Nugæ Canoræ Medicæ.
Lays of the Poet Laureate of the New Town Dispensary. Edited by Professor DOUGLAS MACLAGAN. 4to, with Illustrations, 7s. 6d.

The Hill Forts, Stone Circles, and other Structural Re-
mains of Ancient Scotland. By C. MACLAGAN, Lady Associate of the Society of Antiquaries of Scotland. With Plans and Illustrations. Folio, 31s. 6d.
" We need not enlarge on the few inconsequential speculations which rigid archæologists may find in the present volume. We desire rather to commend it to their careful study, fully assured that not only they, but also the general reader, will be edified by its perusal."—*Scotsman.*

The Light of the World.
By DAVID M'LAREN, Minister of Humbie. Crown 8vo, 6s.

The Book of Psalms in Metre.
According to the version approved of by the Church of Scotland. Revised by Rev. DAVID M'LAREN. Crown 8vo, 7s. 6d.

Omnipotence belongs only to the Beloved.
By Mrs. BREWSTER MACPHERSON. Extra fcap., 3s. 6d.

Humorous Masterpieces from American Literature,
from 1810 to 1886. Edited by EDWARD T. MASON. Selections are made from the Works of : ALCOTT, ALDEN, ALDRICH, BALDWIN, BEECHER, BELLAMY, BROUNE, BUNNER, BUTLER, CABLE, CAVAZZA, CLEMENS, CONE, COZZENS, CRANE, CURTIS, DODGE, DUNNING, HALE, HARTE, HARRIS, HAWTHORNE, HOLMES, HOWE, HOWELLS, IRVING, JOHNSON, LANIGAN, LELAND, LOWELL, LUDLOW, M'DOWELL, MATTHEWS, OGDEN, PHELPS, QUINCEY, ROCHE, SAXE, SEBA, SMITH, STOFFORD, STOCKTON, STOWE, THORPE, THROWBRIDGE, WARNER, Etc. 3 vols. square 16mo, 3s. 6d. each vol.

In Partnership. Studies in Story-Telling.
By BRANDER MATTHEWS and H. C. BUNNER. 1s. in paper, and 2s. in cloth.

Antwerp Delivered in MDLXXVII. :
A Passage from the History of the Netherlands, illustrated with Facsimiles of a rare series of Designs by Martin de Vos, and of Prints by Hogenberg, the Wiericxes, etc. By Sir WILLIAM STIRLING-MAXWELL, Bart., K.T. and M.P. In 1 vol. Folio, 5 guineas.
"A splendid folio in richly ornamented binding, protected by an almost equally ornamental slip-cover. . . . Remarkable illustrations of the manner in which the artists of the time 'pursued their labours in a country ravaged by war, and in cities ever menaced by siege and sack.'"—*Scotsman.*

Studies in the Topography of Galloway, being a List
of nearly 4000 Names of Places, with Remarks on their Origin and Meaning. By SIR HERBERT MAXWELL, Bart., M.P. 1 vol. demy 8vo, 14s.

The History of Old Dundee, narrated out of the Town
Council Register, with Additions from Contemporary Annals. By ALEXANDER MAXWELL, F.S.A. Scot. 4to. Cloth, 21s. ; Roxburghe, 24s.

Researches and Excavations at Carnac (Morbihan),
The Bossenno, and Mont St. Michel. By JAMES MILN. Royal 8vo, with Maps, Plans, and numerous Illustrations in Wood-Engraving and Chromolithography.

Excavations at Carnac (Brittany), a Record of Archæo-
logical Researches in the Alignments of Kermario. By JAMES MILN. Royal 8vo, with Maps, Plans, and numerous Illustrations in Wood-Engraving. 15s.

The Past in the Present—What is Civilisation?
Being the Rhind Lectures in Archæology, delivered in 1876 and 1878. By ARTHUR MITCHELL, C.B., M.D., LL.D., Secretary to the Society of Antiquaries of Scotland. In 1 vol. demy 8vo, with 148 Woodcuts, 15s.
"Whatever differences of opinion, however, may be held on minor points, there can be no question that Dr. Mitchell's work is one of the ablest and most original pieces of archæological literature which has appeared of late years."—*St. James's Gazette.*

In War Time. A Novel. By S. WEIR MITCHELL, M.D. Crown 8vo, 6s.

Roland Blake. A Novel. By S. WEIR MITCHELL, M.D. Crown 8vo, 6s.

Our Scotch Banks :
Their Position and their Policy. By WM. MITCHELL, S.S.C. Third Edition. 8vo, 5s.

On Horse-Breaking.
By ROBERT MORETON. Second Edition. Fcap. 8vo, 1s.

Ecclesiological Notes on some of the Islands of Scot-
land, with other Papers relating to Ecclesiological Remains on the Scottish Mainland and Islands. By THOMAS S. MUIR, Author of "Characteristics of Church Architecture," etc. Demy 8vo, with numerous Illustrations, 21s.

The Birds of Berwickshire.
By Geo. Muirhead. 1 vol. demy 8vo, Illustrated. To Subscribers only.
[*In the Press.*

Ancient Scottish Lake-Dwellings or Crannogs, with a
Supplementary Chapter on Remains of Lake-Dwellings in England. By Robert Munro, M.D., F.S.A. Scot. 1 vol. demy 8vo, profusely illustrated, 21s.

"A standard authority on the subject of which it treats."—*Times.*

". . . Our readers may be assured that they will find very much to interest and instruct them in the perusal of the work."—*Athenæum.*

"The Lanox of Auld:" An Epistolary Review of "The
Lennox, by William Fraser." By Mark Napier. With Woodcuts and Plates. 4to, 15s.

Tenants' Gain not Landlords' Loss, and some other
Economic Aspects of the Land Question. By Joseph Shield Nicholson, M.A., Professor of Political Economy in the University of Edinburgh. Crown 8vo, 5s.

Verses of a Prose Writer.
By Jas. Ashcroft Noble. Fcap. 8vo, price 5s.

Camps in the Caribbees: Adventures of a Naturalist
in the Lesser Antilles. By Frederick Ober. Illustrations, demy 8vo, 12s.

"Well-written and well-illustrated narrative of camping out among the Caribbees."—*Westminster Review.*

"Varied were his experiences, hairbreadth his escapes, and wonderful his gleanings in the way of securing rare birds."—*The Literary World.*

Cookery for the Sick and a Guide for the Sick-Room.
By C. H. Oao, an Edinburgh Nurse. Fcap. 1s.

The Lord Advocates of Scotland from the close of the
Fifteenth Century to the passing of the Reform Bill. By G. W. T. Omond, Advocate. 2 vols. demy 8vo, 28s.

The Arniston Memoirs—Three Centuries of a Scottish
House, 1571-1838. Edited from Family Papers by Geo. W. T. Omond, Advocate. 1 vol. 8vo, 21s., with Etchings, Lithographs, and Woodcuts.

An Irish Garland.
By Mrs. S. M. B. Piatt. Crown 8vo, 3s. 6d.

The Children Out of Doors. A Book of Verses.
By Two in One House. Crown 8vo, 3s. 6d.

Phœbe.
By the Author of "Rutledge." Reprinted from the Fifth Thousand of the American Edition. Crown 8vo, 6s.

"'Phœbe' is a woman's novel."—*Saturday Review.*

Popular Genealogists;
Or, The Art of Pedigree-making. Crown 8vo, 4s.

The Gamekeeper's Manual: being Epitome of the Game
Laws for the use of Gamekeepers and others interested in the Preservation of Game. By Alexander Porter, Deputy Chief Constable of Roxburghshire. Fcap. 8vo, 1s.

Kuram, Kabul, and Kandahar: being a Brief Record of
the Impressions in Three Campaigns under General Roberts. By Lieutenant Robertson, 8th, "The King's," Regiment. Crown 8vo, with Maps, 6s.

Scotland under her Early Kings.
A History of the Kingdom to the close of the 13th century. By E. William Robertson. In 2 vols. 8vo, cloth, 36s.

Historical Essays,
In connection with the Land and the Church, etc. By E. William Robertson, Author of "Scotland under her Early Kings." 8vo, 10s. 6d.

A Rectorial Address delivered before the Students of
Aberdeen University, in the Music Hall at Aberdeen, on Nov. 5, 1880. By THE EARL OF ROSEBERY. 6d.

A Rectorial Address delivered before the Students of
the University of Edinburgh, Nov. 4, 1882. By THE EARL OF ROSEBERY. 6d.

Aberdour and Inchcolme. Being Historical Notices of
the Parish and Monastery, in Twelve Lectures. By the Rev. WILLIAM ROSS, LL.D., Author of "Burgh Life in Dunfermline in the Olden Time." Crown 8vo, 6s.

"If any one would know what Aberdour has been, or, indeed, what to some extent has been the history of many another parish in Scotland, he cannot do better than read these Lectures. He will find the task a pleasant one."—*Saturday Review.*

"We know no book which within so small a compass contains so varied, so accurate, and so vivid a description of the past life of the Scottish people, whether ecclesiastical or social, as Dr. Ross's 'Aberdour and Inchcolme.'"—*Scottish Review.*

"It seems a pity that so good a thing should have been so long withheld from a wider audience; but better late than never."—*Scotsman.*

Notes and Sketches from the Wild Coasts of Nipon.
With Chapters on Cruising after Pirates in Chinese Waters. By HENRY C. ST. JOHN, Captain R.N. Small demy 8vo, with Maps and Illustrations, 12s.

"One of the most charming books of travel that has been published for some time."—*Scotsman.*

"There is a great deal more in the book than Natural History. . . . His pictures of life and manners are quaint and effective, and the more so from the writing being natural and free from effort."—*Athenæum.*

"He writes with a simplicity and directness, and not seldom with a degree of graphic power, which, even apart from the freshness of the matter, renders his book delightful reading. Nothing could be better of its kind than the description of the Inland Sea."—*Daily News.*

Notes on the Natural History of the Province of Moray.
By the late CHARLES ST. JOHN, Author of "Wild Sports in the Highlands." Second Edition. In 1 vol. royal 8vo, with 40 page Illustrations of Scenery and Animal Life, engraved by A. DURAND after sketches made by GEORGE REID, R.S.A., and J. WYCLIFFE TAYLOR; also, 30 Pen-and-Ink Drawings by the Author in facsimile. 50s.

"This is a new edition of the work brought out by the friends of the late Mr. St. John in 1863; but it is so handsomely and nobly printed, and enriched with such charming illustrations, that we may consider it a new book."—*St. James's Gazette.*

"Charles St. John was not an artist, but he had the habit of roughly sketching animals in positions which interested him, and the present reprint is adorned by a great number of these, facsimiled from the author's original pen and ink. Some of these, as for instance the studies of the golden eagle swooping on its prey, and that of the otter swimming with a salmon in its mouth, are very interesting, and full of that charm that comes from the exact transcription of unusual observation."—*Pall Mall Gazette.*

A Tour in Sutherlandshire, with Extracts from the
Field-Books of a Sportsman and Naturalist. By the late CHARLES ST. JOHN, Author of "Wild Sports and Natural History in the Highlands." Second Edition, with an Appendix on the Fauna of Sutherland, by J. A. HARVIE-BROWN and T. E. BUCKLEY. Illustrated with the original Wood Engravings, and additional Vignettes from the Author's sketch-books. In 2 vols. small demy 8vo, 21s.

"Every page is full of interest."—*The Field.*

"There is not a wild creature in the Highlands, from the great stag to the tiny fire-crested wren, of which he has not something pleasant to say."—*Pall Mall Gazette.*

Life of James Hepburn, Earl of Bothwell.
By Professor SCHIERN, Copenhagen. Translated from the Danish by the Rev. DAVID BERRY, F.S.A. Scot. Demy 8vo, 16s.

Scotch Folk.
Illustrated. Fourth Edition enlarged. Ex. fcap. 8vo, 1s.

"They are stories of the best type, quite equal in the main to the average of Dean Ramsay's well-known collection."—*Aberdeen Free Press.*

Studies in Poetry and Philosophy.
By the late J. C. SHAIRP, LL.D., Principal of the United College of St. Salvator and St. Leonard, St. Andrews. Fourth Edition, with Portraits of the Author and Thomas Erskine, by WILLIAM HOLE, A.R.S.A. Crown 8vo, 7s. 6d.

"In the 'Moral Dynamic,' Mr. Shairp seeks for something which shall persuade us of the vital and close bearing on each other of moral thought and spiritual energy. It is this conviction which has animated Mr. Shairp in every page of the volume before us. It is because he appreciates so justly and forcibly the powers of philosophic doctrine over all the field of human life, that he leans with such strenuous trust upon those ideas which Wordsworth unsystematically, and Coleridge more systematically, made popular and fertile among us."—*Saturday Review.*

"The finest essay in the volume, partly because it is upon the greatest and most definite subject, is the first, on *Wordsworth.* . . . We have said so much upon this essay that we can only say of the other three that they are fully worthy to stand beside it."—*Spectator.*

Culture and Religion.
By the late PRINCIPAL SHAIRP. Seventh Edition. Fcap. 8vo, 3s. 6d.

"A wise book, and, unlike a great many other wise books, has that carefully shaded/thought and expression which fits Professor Shairp to speak for Culture no less than for Religion."—*Spectator.*

"Those who remember a former work of Principal Shairp's, 'Studies in Poetry and Philosophy,' will feel secure that all which comes from his pen will bear the marks of thought, at once careful, liberal, and accurate. Nor will they be disappointed in the present work. . . . We can recommend this book to our readers."—*Athenæum.*

"We cannot close without earnestly recommending the book to thoughtful young men. It combines the loftiest intellectual power with a simple and childlike faith in Christ, and exerts an influence which must be stimulating and healthful."—*Freeman.*

Sketches in History and Poetry.
By the late PRINCIPAL SHAIRP. Edited by JOHN VEITCH, Professor of Logic and Rhetoric in the University of Glasgow. Crown 8vo. 7s. 6d.

Kilmahoe, a Highland Pastoral,
And other Poems. By PRINCIPAL SHAIRP. Fcap. 8vo, 6s.

Shakespeare on Golf. With special Reference to St.
Andrews Links. 3d.

The Divine Comedy of Dante Alighieri, The Inferno.
A Translation in Terza Rima, with Notes and Introductory Essay. By JAMES ROMANES SIBBALD. With an Engraving after Giotto's Portrait. Small demy 8vo, 12s.

"Mr. Sibbald is certainly to be congratulated on having produced a translation which would probably give an English reader a better conception of the nature of the original poem, having regard both to its matter and its form in combination, than any other English translation yet published."—*Academy.*

The Use of what is called Evil.
A Discourse by SIMPLICIUS. Extracted from his Commentary on the Enchiridion of Epictetus. Crown 8vo, 1s.

The Near and the Far View,
And other Sermons. By Rev. A. L. SIMPSON, D.D., Derby. Ex. fcap. 8vo, 5s.

"Very fresh and thoughtful are these sermons."—*Literary World.*

"Dr. Simpson's sermons may fairly claim distinctive power. He looks at things with his own eyes, and often shows us what with ordinary vision we had failed to perceive. . . . The sermons are distinctively good."—*British Quarterly Review.*

Archæological Essays.

By the late Sir JAMES SIMPSON, Bart. Edited by the late JOHN STUART, LL.D. 2 vols. 4to, 21s.

1. Archæology.
2. Inchcolm.
3. The Cat Stane.
4. Magical Charm-Stones.
5. Pyramid of Gizeh.
6. Leprosy and Leper Hospitals.
7. Greek Medical Vases.
8. Was the Roman Army provided with Medical Officers?
9. Roman Medicine Stamps, etc. etc.

The Art of Golf.

By SIR W. G. SIMPSON, Bart., Captain of the Honourable Company of Edinburgh Golfers. With Twenty Plates from instantaneous photographs of Professional Players, chiefly by A. F. Macfie, Esq. Demy 8vo, Morocco back, price 15s.

The Four Ancient Books of Wales,

Containing the Cymric Poems attributed to the Bards of the sixth century. By WILLIAM F. SKENE, D.C.L., Historiographer-Royal for Scotland. With Maps and Facsimiles. 2 vols. 8vo, 36s.

Celtic Scotland: A History of Ancient Alban.

By WILLIAM F. SKENE, D.C.L., Historiographer-Royal for Scotland. In 3 vols. Demy 8vo, 45s. Illustrated with Maps.

I.—HISTORY and ETHNOLOGY. II.—CHURCH and CULTURE.
III.—LAND and PEOPLE.

"Forty years ago Mr. Skene published a small historical work on the Scottish Highlands which has ever since been appealed to as an authority, but which has long been out of print. The promise of this youthful effort is amply fulfilled in the three weighty volumes of his maturer years. As a work of historical research it ought in our opinion to take a very high rank."— *Times.*

The Gospel History for the Young:

Being lessons on the Life of Christ, Adapted for use in Families and Sunday Schools. By WILLIAM F. SKENE, D.C.L., Historiographer-Royal for Scotland. Small crown 8vo, 3 vols., with Maps, 5s. each vol., or in cloth box, 15s.

"In a spirit altogether unsectarian provides for the young a simple, interesting, and thoroughly charming history of our Lord."—*Literary World.*

"This 'Gospel History for the Young' is one of the most valuable books of the kind."—*The Churchman.*

Shelley: a Critical Biography.

By GEORGE BARNETT SMITH. Ex. fcap. 8vo, 6s.

The Sermon on the Mount.

By the Rev. WALTER C. SMITH, D.D. Crown 8vo, 6s.

Life and Work at the Great Pyramid.

With a Discussion of the Facts ascertained. By C. PIAZZI SMYTH, F.R.SS.L. and E., Astronomer-Royal for Scotland. 3 vols. Demy 8vo, 56s.

Madeira Meteorologic:

Being a Paper on the above subject read before the Royal Society, Edinburgh, on the 1st of May 1882. By C. PIAZZI SMYTH, Astronomer-Royal for Scotland. Small 4to, 6s.

Saskatchewan and the Rocky Mountains.

Diary and Narrative of Travel, Sport, and Adventure, during a Journey through part of the Hudson's Bay Company's Territories in 1859 and 1860. By the EARL OF SOUTHESK, K.T., F.R.G.S. 1 vol. demy 8vo, with Illustrations on Wood by WHYMPER, 18s.

By the same Author.

Herminius:

A Romance. Fcap. 8vo, 6s.

Jonas Fisher:

A Poem in Brown and White. Cheap Edition. 1s.

The Burial of Isis and other Poems.
Fcap. 8vo, 6s.

Darroll, and other Poems.
By WALTER COOK SPENS, Advocate.   Crown 8vo, 5s.

Rudder Grange.
By FRANK R. STOCKTON.   1s. ; and cloth, 2s.

"'Rudder Grange' is a book that few could produce, and that most would be proud to sign."—*Saturday Review.*

"It may be safely recommended as a very amusing little book."—*Athenæum.*

"Altogether 'Rudder Grange' is as cheery, as humorous, and as wholesome a little story as we have read for many a day."—*St. James's Gazette.*

"The minutest incidents are narrated with such genuine humour and gaiety, that at the close of the volume the reader is sorry to take leave of the merry innocent party."—*Westminster Review.*

The Lady or the Tiger? and other Stories.
By FRANK R. STOCKTON.   1s. ; and cloth, 2s.

Contents.—The Lady or the Tiger?—The Transferred Ghost—The Spectral Mortgage—That same old 'Coon—His Wife's Deceased Sister—Mr. Tolman—Plain Fishing—My Bull Calf—Every Man his own Letter Writer—The Remarkable Wreck of the "Thomas Hyke."

"Stands by itself both for originality of plot and freshness of humour."—*Century Magazine.*

A Borrowed Month, and other Stories.
By FRANK R. STOCKTON, Author of "Rudder Grange."   1s. ; and cloth, 2s.

Contents.—A Borrowed Month—A Tale of Negative Gravity—The Christmas Wreck—Our Archery Club—A Story of Assisted Fate—The Discourager of Hesitancy—Our Story.

Christianity Confirmed by Jewish and Heathen Testimony, and the Deductions from Physical Science, etc. By THOMAS STEVENSON, F.R.S.E., F.G.S., Member of the Institution of Civil Engineers. Second Edition. Fcap. 8vo, 3s. 6d.

What is Play?
A Physiological Inquiry. Its bearing upon Education and Training. By JOHN STRACHAN, M.D. Fcap., 1s.

Good Lives: Some Fruits of the Nineteenth Century.
By A. M. SYMINGTON, D.D. Small crown 8vo, 3s. 6d.

Sketch of Thermodynamics.
By P. G. TAIT, Professor of Natural Philosophy in the University of Edinburgh. Second Edition, revised and extended. Crown 8vo, 5s.

Talks with our Farm-Servants.
By An Old Farm-Servant. Crown 8vo ; paper, 6d. ; cloth, 1s.

Walden; or, Life in the Woods.
By H. D. THOREAU. Crown 8vo, 6s.

Tommie Brown and the Queen of the Fairies; a new
Child's Book, in fcap. 8vo. With Illustrations, 4s. 6d.

Let pain be pleasure, and pleasure be pain.

"There is no wonder that children liked the story. It is told neatly and well, and is full of great cleverness, while it has that peculiar character the absence of which from many like stories deprives them of any real interest for children."—*Scotsman.*

Our Mission to the Court of Marocco in 1880, under
Sir JOHN DRUMMOND HAY, K.C.B., Minister Plenipotentiary at Tangier, and Envoy Extraordinary to His Majesty the Sultan of Marocco. By Captain PHILIP DURHAM TROTTER, 93d Highlanders. Illustrated from Photographs by the Hon. D. LAWLESS, Rifle Brigade. Square Demy 8vo, 24s.

The Upland Tarn: A Village Idyll.
Small Crown, 5s.

Mr. Washington Adams in England.

By RICHARD GRANT WHITE. 1s.; or in cloth, 2s.

"An impudent book."—*Vanity Fair.*

"This short, tiresome book."—*Saturday Review.*

"Brimful of genuine humour."—*Montrose Standard.*

"Mr. White is a capital caricaturist, but in portraying the ludicrous eccentricities of the patrician Britisher he hardly succeeds so well as in delineating the peculiar charms of the representative Yankee."—*Whitehall Review.*

Rosetty Ends, or the Chronicles of a Country Cobbler.

By Job Bradawl (A. DEWAR WILLOCK), Author of "She Noddit to me." Fcap. 8vo, Illustrated. 2s.

"The sketches are amusing productions, narrating comical incidents, connected by a thread of common character running through them all—a thread waxed into occasional strength by the 'roset' of a homely, entertaining wit."—*Scotsman.*

The Botany of Three Historical Records:

Pharaoh's Dream, the Sower, and the King's Measure. By A. STEPHEN WILSON. Crown 8vo, with 5 Plates, 3s. 6d.

"A Bushel of Corn."

By A. STEPHEN WILSON. An investigation by Experiments into all the more important questions which range themselves round a Bushel of Wheat, a Bushel of Barley, and a Bushel of Oats. Crown 8vo, with Illustrations, 9s.

"It is full of originality and force."—*Nature.*

"A monument of painstaking research."—*Liverpool Mercury.*

"Mr. Wilson's book is interesting not only for agriculturists and millers, but for all who desire information on the subject of corn, in which every one is so intimately concerned."—*Morning Post.*

Songs and Poems.

By A. STEPHEN WILSON. Crown 8vo, 6s.

Reminiscences of Old Edinburgh.

By DANIEL WILSON, LL.D., F.R.S.E., Professor of History and English Literature in University College, Toronto, Author of "Prehistoric Annals of Scotland," etc. etc. 2 vols. post 8vo, 15s.

The India Civil Service as a Career for Scotsmen.

By J. WILSON, M.A. 1s.

Christianity and Reason:

Their necessary connection. By R. S. WYLD, LL.D. Extra fcap. 8vo, 3s. 6d.

Shakespeare's England.

By WILLIAM WINTER. 1s., paper, or 2s., cloth extra.

Contents.—The Voyage—The Beauty of England—Great Historic Places—Rambles in London—A Visit to Windsor—The Palace of Westminster—Warwick and Kenilworth—First View of Stratford-on-Avon—London Nooks and Corners—Relics of Lord Byron—Westminster Abbey—The Home of Shakespeare—Up to London—Old Churches of London—Literary Shrines of London—A Haunt of Edmund Kean—Stoke-Pogis and Thomas Gray—At the Grave of Coleridge—On Barnet Battlefield—A Glimpse of Canterbury—The Shrines of Warwickshire—A Borrower of the Night.

The East Neuk of Fife: its History and Antiquities.

Second Edition, Re-arranged and Enlarged. By the Rev. WALTER WOOD, M.A., Elie. Edited, with Preface and Index, by the Rev. J. WOOD BROWN, M.A., Gordon. Crown 8vo. 6s.

EDINBURGH: DAVID DOUGLAS, CASTLE STREET.

www.ingramcontent.com/pod-product-compliance
Lightning Source LLC
Chambersburg PA
CBHW030849270326
41928CB00008B/1291